The Australian Geographic Book of

The Kimberley

by David McGonigal

PUBLISHER & EDITOR-IN-CHIEF
DICK SMITH

CHIEF EXECUTIVE
IKE BAIN

MANAGING EDITOR
HOWARD WHELAN

EDITOR
DAVID McGONIGAL

PRINCIPAL PHOTOGRAPHER
ROBBI NEWMAN

ART DIRECTOR
TONY GORDON

SERIES DESIGNER
KEN GILROY

DIRECTOR OF CARTOGRAPHY
WILL PRINGLE

Cover: Piccaninny Creek, Bungle Bungle Range by Robbi Newman.

Back cover: Chinatown, Broome.

Previous page: the sun setting behind a boab tree at Derby.

First published 1990

Published by Australian Geographic Pty Ltd
for the Australian Geographic Society
PO Box 321, Terrey Hills,
NSW 2084, Australia
© Copyright Australian Geographic Pty Ltd 1990
Printed in Australia by Inprint
Typeset by The Typographers

National Library of Australia
Cataloguing-in-Publication Data:
McGonigal, David, 1950– ,
The Australian Geographic Book of
The Kimberley.

Bibliography
Includes index

ISBN 1 86276 005 5
1. Kimberley (WA) – History. 2. Kimberley (WA)
– Description and travel. I. Title

994.14

Acknowledgements
The editor would like to thank the people of the
Kimberley who gave their time unstintingly,
providing information and assistance during
the lengthy research process and later in
checking the manuscript. In particular, thanks
must go to Chris Done, regional manager of
CALM, the MacDonald family of Fossil Downs,
Dame Mary Durack Miller, the WA Tourism Commission, the Shire Councils of the region, Ian
Elliot, who checked the nomenclature, and
Frank Povah who proofread the manuscript.
Special thanks must go to Cathie Clement,
whose wonderfully detailed knowledge of
early European settlement of the Kimberley
was invaluable.

Photo credits are on page 159.

Publisher's Introduction

Ever since I read Hans Bertram's *Flight into Hell* many years ago, I've been fascinated by the Kimberley. Bertram's book tells an extraordinary tale of survival that took place on the Kimberley's north coast in 1932. Bertram and his mechanic, Adolph Klausmann, were flying their Junkers seaplane *Atlantis* from Timor to Darwin when they lost their way. Short of fuel, they were forced to land in an inlet about 160 kilometres north-west of Wyndham. This was the start of a 38-day nightmare of privation as they vainly searched for human habitation. The ordeal ended when they were found by an Aborigine from the Drysdale River Mission.

However, it was the investigation of an aviation incident that had taken place three years before this that first brought me to the region. In 1981, I organised an expedition that found the spot where, in 1929, Charles Kingsford Smith made the forced landing that sparked what came to be known as the "Coffee Royal" affair.

What made the Kimberley appear so exotic to me was the fact that here was an expanse of land so enormous it covered a greater area than even some countries, yet it had a population smaller than that of many a country town. Even after everything I'd read about the Kimberley, when I first saw it I was struck as much by its grandeur as by the harshness it still imposes on its inhabitants. It would be hard to think of a place more worthy of the title of "the last frontier".

So when the success of the AUSTRALIAN GEOGRAPHIC journal led naturally to the idea of publishing a series of books, it was fitting that one on the Kimberley should be the first commissioned. Our aim is to produce inexpensive books packed with information and illustrated with stunning photographs. David McGonigal has written for AUSTRALIAN GEOGRAPHIC from the early days and visiting the Kimberley for articles on the Bungle Bungle Range and Maxine MacDonald fired his enthusiasm for the Kimberley book project. He became both editor and principal author of *The Australian Geographic Book of The Kimberley*. David, photographer Robbi Newman – who has been to the region on several occasions – and pilot Rob Thompson flew a light plane from Sydney to the Kimberley for a fresh look at the whole area.

Dr Bob Young of the University of Wollongong did a lot of early research work on Purnululu (Bungle Bungle) National Park and has specialised in the geography of the Kimberley. He has written "An Ancient Land", the chapter that explains the fascinating landforms of the Kimberley. Kim Akerman was there when the Kimberley Land Council was formed and has been closely involved with the Aborigines of the Kimberley for many years. Kim, who is an expert in Aboriginal art and customs, is now with the Darwin Museum and Art Gallery; he wrote "The Original Inhabitants". Besides "European Explorers" and "Early European Settlement", Cathie Clement's contributions pop up throughout the book. Cathie is a professional historian who has spent most of her academic life studying the Kimberley and unravelling facts from the fables that have arisen in over a century of European settlement.

Since I first visited this north-west corner of our continent, I've been back every year, many times on holidays with my family. I think it's a very special place and I hope that through this book you'll discover the wonder of that part of Australia known simply as "the Kimberley".

Dick Smith
Publisher

Dick Smith bushwalking in the Kimberley.

Contents

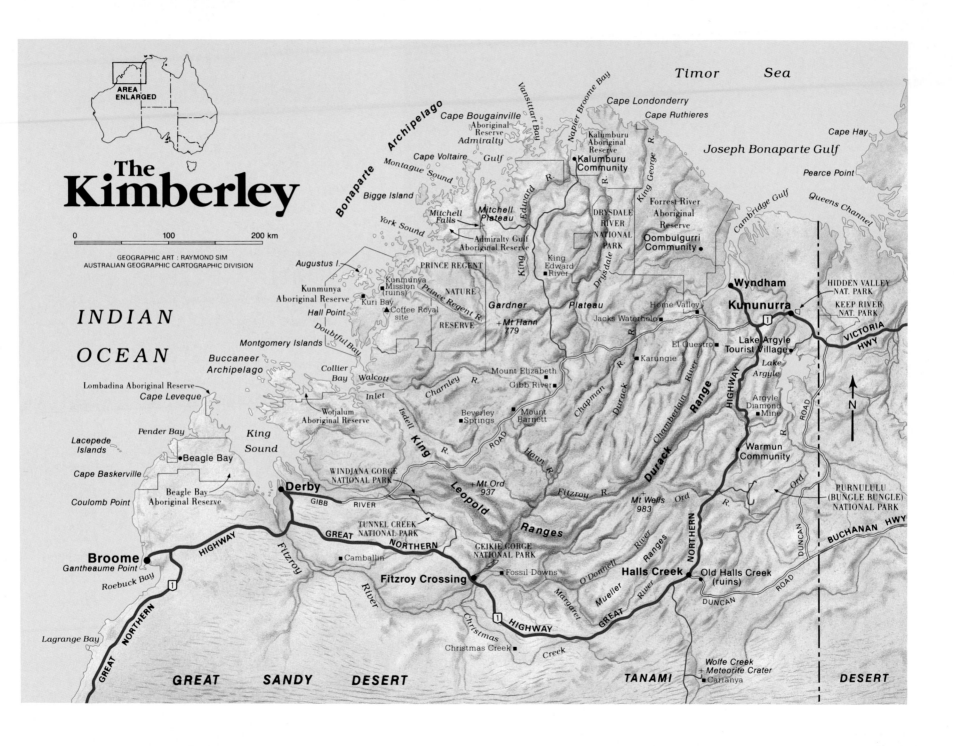

The Kimberley

GEOGRAPHIC ART : RAYMOND SIM
AUSTRALIAN GEOGRAPHIC CARTOGRAPHIC DIVISION

0   100   200 km

AREA ENLARGED

Timor Sea

Indian Ocean

Joseph Bonaparte Gulf

Cape Londonderry
Cape Ruthieres
Cape Hay
Pearce Point
Queens Channel
Cambridge Gulf
Napier Broome Bay
Vansittart Bay

Cape Bougainville
Aboriginal Reserve
Admiralty Gulf
Cape Voltaire
Montague Sound
Bigge Island
York Sound
Mitchell Falls
Mitchell Plateau

Kalumburu Aboriginal Reserve
Kalumburu Community
Forrest River Aboriginal Reserve
Oombulgurri Community

Bonaparte Archipelago

DRYSDALE RIVER NATIONAL PARK

King Edward R.
King George R.
Drysdale R.

Wyndham
HIDDEN VALLEY NAT. PARK
Kununurra
KEEP RIVER NAT. PARK
VICTORIA HWY

Augustus I.
Kunmunya Mission (ruins)
Kunmunya Aboriginal Reserve
Hall Point
Kuri Bay
Coffee Royal site
Doubtful Bay

PRINCE REGENT
NATURE
RESERVE
Prince Regent R.
Gardner
+ Mt Hann 779

Plateau
Home Valley
Jacks Waterhole
El Questro
Karungie

Lake Argyle Tourist Village
Lake Argyle

Montgomery Islands
Collier Bay
Walcott Inlet
Wotjalum Aboriginal Reserve

Buccaneer Archipelago

Lombadina Aboriginal Reserve
Cape Leveque

Lacepede Islands
Pender Bay
Beagle Bay

Cape Baskerville
Beagle Bay Aboriginal Reserve
Coulomb Point

King Sound

Mount Elizabeth
Gibb River
Charnley R.
Beverley Springs
Mount Barnett

Chapman R.
Durack R.
Chamberlain River

Durack Range

Argyle Diamond Mine

N

Warmun Community

PURNULULU (BUNGLE BUNGLE) NATIONAL PARK

Isdell R.
King R.
ROAD
Hann R.

+ Mt Ord 937

Leopold Ranges

WINDJANA GORGE NATIONAL PARK
Derby
GIBB RIVER

TUNNEL CREEK NATIONAL PARK
GEIKIE GORGE NATIONAL PARK

GREAT NORTHERN

Fitzroy R.
+ Mt Wells 983

Ord R.

NORTHERN HIGHWAY

BUCHANAN HWY

Broome
Gantheaume Point
Roebuck Bay
HIGHWAY

Fitzroy River
Camballin

Fossil Downs
Fitzroy Crossing

O'Donnell R.
Mueller River
Margaret River
Ranges

Halls Creek
Old Halls Creek (ruins)

DUNCAN ROAD

GREAT

1

HIGHWAY

Christmas Creek
Christmas Creek

Lagrange Bay

GREAT   SANDY   DESERT

TANAMI

Wolfe Creek + Meteorite Crater
Carranya

DESERT

Introduction

by David McGonigal

WE TOOK off from Derby mid-morning and flew across King Sound towards the sea. As we turned north towards Kalumburu, the land and seascape that unfolded below us was awe-inspiring. Hundreds of craggy brown islands, some covering many hectares and others only a few square metres, were scattered across the sea in a maze that appeared to have been deliberately set for mariners. Where land and water met, there were empty beaches and rocky headlands; the outgoing tide left a line of foam as it swept towards the deep water, trailing eddies, whirlpools and whitecaps. Apart from the isolated mining community on Koolan Island and the resort of Cockatoo Island, we saw not a single trace of human habitation in the five-hour flight. Elsewhere in the world, this scenery would attract thousands of tourists. But this is the remote Kimberley, so few even know of its existence.

Flying over the Kimberley affords a glimpse into the very essence of Australia. More than that, it's a glimpse of what the world was like when it was young. From high above, the twisted rock strata form intricate patterns, the original shapes of a now ancient land laid bare by millennia of erosion. There's no predominance of mountains, rivers, forests, beaches, plains or grasslands. Rather, it's a mixture of all these, forming an integrated whole – the region called "the Kimberley".

The Aborigines of the Kimberley are the descendants of people who walked upon this land more than 40,000 years ago when Australia was still joined to New Guinea. They were here during the last Ice Age and had to move when the shoreline advanced 200 kilometres into the Timor Sea and then receded as the world's oceans alternately froze into the polar ice caps and melted again. Today, there is a spirit of enthusiasm in the Aboriginal communities of the north-west as the original Australians develop a role in modern Australia which doesn't require them to renounce their ancient culture. This is reflected in a growing interest in Kimberley Aboriginal art.

The Kimberley is an enigma. It is one of the oldest parts of the most ancient continent on Earth, with a continuous population from not long after the dawn of humankind, yet most of its white history is within living memory. Here, the first days of European settlement aren't relegated to dry history texts: they are events experienced by the parents and grandparents of people living in the Kimberley today.

(Contents page) In this ungainly take-off from Marlgu Billabong near Wyndham, a pelican reveals the difficulty of launching its bulk into the air. Once airborne, however, pelicans are skilful and graceful fliers. Weighing on average 5 kg and capable of reaching 8 kg, Australian pelicans are ubiquitous and the largest of the family Pelecanidae, a family found throughout the world. William Dampier noted the Kimberley pelican population in 1699.

(Following page) A symphony in corrugated iron, this house in Broome, with its wide verandahs built to collect any breeze, reveals the architectural style that has evolved to suit Australia's tropics. Before the age of air-conditioning, home life revolved around the verandah, the coolest part of the house. Corrugated iron, a mainstay of Australian rural construction, was first produced in Australia at Darling Harbour, NSW, in the 1870s but its aesthetic qualities have only been recognised in recent years.

Although this is the part of Australia closest to our most populous neighbours (and was possibly visited by seafarers from Asia for centuries before any European vessel ventured to the east coast), it is regarded as the most isolated because it is the most distant from the main population centres on the eastern seaboard. Just arriving in the Kimberley feels like an achievement, yet the real adventure lies ahead.

It is this isolation that has allowed the Kimberley region to maintain a rugged individuality distinct from the rest of the country and yet remain typically Australian.

The Kimberley is the north-west corner of the Australian continent. Its boundaries are the Timor Sea and the Indian Ocean to the north and west, and the Great Sandy Desert to the south. The eastern boundary is arbitrarily fixed as the Northern Territory border. Even so, the Kimberley region looks quite different from any part of the NT east of the Victoria River.

Mind-numbing statistics about the size of the Kimberley abound. With an area of about 345,350 square kilometres, the region is slightly smaller than Japan (372,000 sq. km) and much larger than the United Kingdom (244,000 sq. km), New Zealand (268,000 sq. km) or the State of Victoria (227,620 sq. km). Yet in this vast area there are only three towns with populations over 2000 and a total population of about 23,000. There's only one main road, the Great Northern Highway, and the section between Fitzroy Crossing and Halls Creek was the last part of Australia's Highway One to be tar-sealed. That was in 1986.

The region was named in 1880 by the Western Australian Government after the Earl of Kimberley, who was British Secretary of State for the Colonies at the time.

Until recently it was sometimes referred to as "the Kimberleys" and there was a strong demarcation between east and west Kimberley. There was a clear historical basis for this division. When continuous settlement of the area by white Australians first took place, some west Kimberley land was taken up by sheep graziers from the south of Western Australia and the eastern part was occupied by cattlemen from the eastern colonies, Queensland, New South Wales and Victoria. Soon afterwards the colony became self-governing and the division was reinforced politically by the splitting of

the region into two electorates. There was strong rivalry between the two regions that has only really broken down over the past decade with improved communication and the end of the Kimberley sheep industry. The last sheep station closed its gates in 1974.

Life in the Kimberley has always been hard. It is difficult to envisage the incredible courage and tenacity of those early pioneers – particularly the MacDonalds and Duracks, who arrived here in 1885 after several years droving their cattle from the eastern colonies. By settling the country's last major grazing area, those early pioneers were filling in the final piece of the picture of European Australia.

However, as in much of the New World, it was the lure of gold that brought the first large influx of Europeans (some 10,000 of them) to the Kimberley. When the Kimberley goldfields (around Halls Creek) came to nothing in 1887, only two years after they were discovered, not everyone left. Those who stayed provided the nucleus for development and their towns continued to service the outlying population.

The history of the Kimberley has been one of slow consolidation rather than rapid development. That's not surprising in a part of the world where nature has been remarkably reluctant to give any encouragement to those presumptuous enough to seek a living from the land. The Ord River Scheme, first investigated in 1941, has yet to realise half its potential. As each new crop was tried, a new predator arose: magpie geese bred in astounding numbers to devour the rice crops, caterpillars ate the cotton and green vegetable bugs attacked the legumes. Only now are the farms of the Ord River Irrigation Area reporting the sort of success that will encourage others to take up the remaining land.

The distance from markets and the difficulties in reaching them has always plagued the cattle and sheep industries of the Kimberley. This is an area where it is almost impossible to travel during the several months of the wet season, far less move stock. Even when the roads are open, the closest markets are at least 2200 km away in Perth or more than 3500 km away in Brisbane, Melbourne or Sydney.

Even the first early runaway success, the Broome pearling industry, had its disastrous setbacks, like those caused by the cyclones of 1887 and

1910 which destroyed many luggers and killed their crews.

But the indications are that the time of the Kimberley has arrived. Sydney was first linked to London by direct telephone in 1930, yet many homes in the Kimberley only joined the national telephone grid in the 1980s. The recent final sealing of the highway removed a large psychological barrier for the traveller. Now tourists are arriving in unprecedented numbers to see the wonders of this region. In a way, the remoteness and isolation that hindered development proved a boon because visitors now come to the Kimberley from the cities to seek the past. Broome is seeing its first renaissance since the decline of the pearling industry in the 1940s as it develops into an important holiday centre. On the other side of the Kimberley, travellers pour into Kununurra on their way to the new national park at the Bungle Bungle Range, one of Australia's most intriguing.

There is also considerable mineral development throughout the Kimberley. The Argyle Diamond Mine, which began operation in 1983, extracts about six tonnes of diamonds a year. That makes it the largest such mine in the world, producing about 37 per cent of the world's diamonds. The restricted-access township for the high-technology mine looks like a huge tourist complex (complete with designer shade-sails over the swimming pool) near the foot of the Ragged Range.

Most who visit the Kimberley develop a fascination for the countryside and the people who live here. Longstanding residents can't imagine living anywhere else. It's a beautiful part of the country that in many ways epitomises the image of Australia that Australians like to present to the world.

Sand, mangroves and mud create abstract patterns in the delta of the Fitzroy River on the shores of King Sound. Early European explorers discovered travel here can be very difficult – there are no deep channels for boats and little firm land for walking. The wet, muddy conditions create other hazards, too: Commander John Wickham's survey expedition named a nearby promontory Point Torment in February 1838 following attacks by swarms of voracious mosquitoes.

An Ancient Land

by Dr Bob Young

More than anywhere else in Australia, the Kimberley is a region that calls upon us to examine the origins of our continent. For here the bones of the land are exposed to even the most casual observer and it is a land of geological curiosities: fossil reefs and flooded mountains, mesas (known locally as "jump-ups") and sandstone spires, a desert meteorite crater and ancient folded mountains. These features are not interrupted by cities, small farms or a dense cover of vegetation. Here the land is all there is.

Geological evidence suggests that the Earth and other planets were created 4600 million years ago. This figure, like so many in geology, challenges the limits of human comprehension but, flicking through millions of years like the days on a desk diary, a fascinating picture emerges of how today's landscape came about.

The oldest rocks in the Kimberley were formed around 1900–2000 million years ago and, apart from some younger ones on the southern margins of

the region, virtually all the rocks of the Kimberley are more than 400 million years old. To put that in perspective, until 200 million years ago all the world's landmasses were part of a single super-continent called Pangaea (meaning "all lands").

If it were only the rocks of the Kimberley that were so old, Australia would have no claim to the title of oldest continent – many parts of the world have ancient rocks. But the Kimberley (and much of Western Australia) is special because there has been little geological activity since most of the rocks were formed. Not only are the rocks of great antiquity but so are the landscapes cut from them.

The last period of intense mountain building in the Kimberley was a staggering 1700 million years ago. Few of the rocks that were formed 500–400 million years ago show signs of subsequent deformation. That makes them old indeed when you consider that the Himalayas are only 4 million years old

Ridges and hills dominate the landscape as you look up Piccaninny Creek towards the Bungle Bungle massif. Virtually unknown a decade ago, the Bungle Bungle Range 40 km south-east of Warmun Community is one of the fastest developing areas of tourist interest in WA.

Like teeth on a saw blade, the bedding planes of the Osmand Range clearly show the tilted rock strata. This type of sandstone formation is known to geographers as a "hog-back".

(formed when the Indian subcontinent collided with Asia) and even the oldest parts of the ocean basins are only 100 million years old. When compared with the mobility of most of the Earth's crust, Australia is indeed a timeless land.

The Kimberley is made up of five geological areas and fringed by one more (see map on this page). The heartland is the Kimberley Basin, an enormous raised thickness of sandstones, shales and basalts which have only been subjected to minor faulting and warping since they were formed between 1800 and 1650 million years ago.

The King Leopold and Halls Creek Orogens on the flanks of the Kimberley Basin are areas of intense folding and faulting (an "orogen" is the eroded remnants of mountain belts). The sedimentary and volcanic rocks of these zones were altered greatly by the heat and pressure of the mountain-building forces and great masses of granitic rocks have risen from deep in the crust. However, all this happened in the distant past, about 1800 million years ago.

Sediment eroded from the older rocks was swept into several large basins around the orogens. These basins are the parts of the region with which most travellers are familiar, for the limestones and sandstones made from those deposits have been carved into the spectacular landforms for which the Kimberley is renowned. They also contain the Kimberley's best cattle country – especially on the great basalt plateaus and plains of the eastern part of the Ord Basin.

Today, it's hard to imagine the hot, arid landscape of the Kimberley buried under glaciers. However, it was, in two glacial ages 700 and 600 million years ago, at a time when the whole continent was much farther south than it is today. There is clear evidence of this in Moonlight Valley to the east of Warmun Commu-

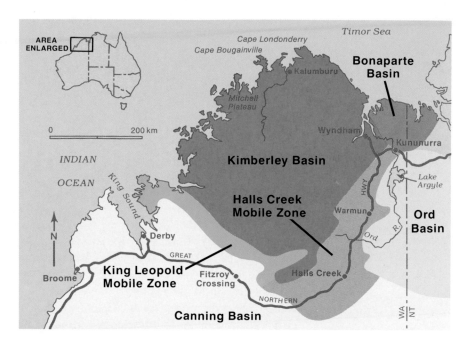

nity and also in the Charnley and Lennard river areas in the western part of the Kimberley. Here very large boulders have been transported almost 50 km from the nearest outcrop of the same rock. And in Moonlight Valley there are highly polished rock fragments and pebbles with the distinctive grooving of glacially transported debris.

By 400 million years ago, the continent had moved north: the Kimberley was in the tropics and much of the lowland was under water. One of the remnants of that time is to be found on the edge of the Canning Basin: some of the best fossil reefs in the world. Today the reefs appear as narrow limestone ranges rising 100 m or so above the surrounding plains. The best known is the Napier Range, especially where the structure of the ancient reef is beautifully exposed in the walls of Windjana Gorge. Geikie Gorge provides a

(Above) The geological zones of the Kimberley region.

(Right) Elaborate concentric banding in fine-grained sandstone from Mount Jowlaenga quarry bears a close resemblance to an Aboriginal ochre painting. Rock from the quarry 80 km due west of Derby on the Dampier Land peninsula has been extracted and cut by Dario De Biasi of Kimberley Colourstone in Derby since 1971.

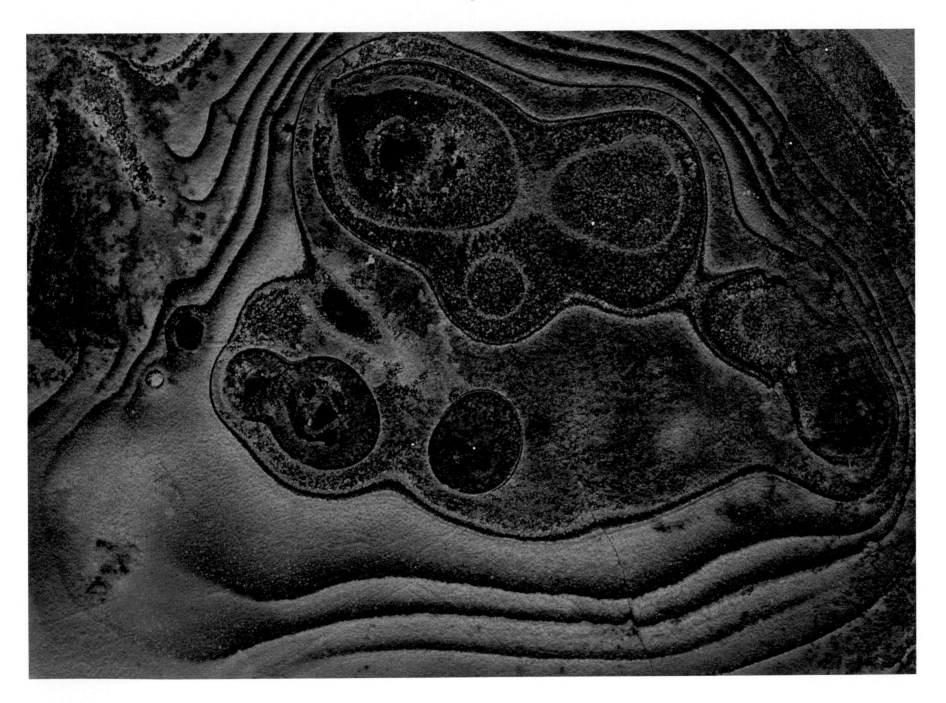

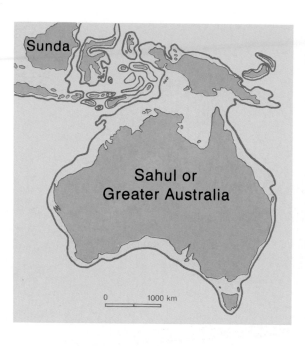

(Above) Fluctuations in sea level have been extensive over the past 100,000 years. This is the Greater Australian land mass above sea level 53,000 years ago.

similar cross-section of the ancient reef. Another, but less spectacular, fossil reef is the Ningbing Limestone north of Kununurra.

The weather was far from stable in those ancient times – there were great fluctuations in climate over the millions of years. Glacial deposits in the Grant Range, near the lower reaches of the Fitzroy River, show that very cold climates prevailed again about 250 million years ago. But over the past 100 million years, the Kimberley climate has been consistently warm to hot. The most spectacular evidence of this is at Gantheaume Point outside Broome, where the footprints of a warm-climate reptile, the dinosaur, have been perfectly preserved in sandstone for about 100 million years.

Until about 30 million years ago, the climatic conditions in the region were much wetter than they are today: there is fossil evidence of widespread rainforests. However, in another reversal, the sand dunes along the southern edges of the Kimberley are evidence of very dry conditions in the near past, within the last few hundred thousand years.

The last very dry spell was only about 20,000 years ago. At that time, with much of the water of the planet's oceans trapped in enlarged polar ice-caps, the sea was more than 100 m below its present level. The very broad and shallow continental shelf of the Timor Sea was not under water then, so the shoreline was 200 km farther out than it is today. The dry conditions and shift in the shoreline resulted in a considerable shift in the distribution of the Aboriginal population.

The most recent melting of the polar ice-caps and the consequent rising of the sea flooded a vast area of lowland beyond the plateau escarp-

(Left) Nestled between Roebuck Bay (foreground) and the Indian Ocean (distant), Broome – the "Port of Pearls" – is the only Kimberley town with a beach. However, until 6000 years ago, the site of Broome wasn't even on the coast. During the last Ice Age, 20,000 years ago, the sea-level was 100 m lower and the shoreline 200 km farther out than it is today. It was only as the climate warmed that the water rose to the current level. The Roebuck Bay side of Broome is characterised by tidal mudflats and mangroves; the wide sandy beach is on the Indian Ocean side.

(Right) Dubbed "China Wall" by the local community and bearing a passing resemblance to its namesake, this natural rock wall 6 km from Halls Creek is claimed to be part of the longest quartz reef in the world.

ment that today forms the spectacular northern coastline of Western Australia. The numerous long inlets along the coast are drowned valleys, while the many offshore islands are all that remain of hills that rose above ancient lowlands.

The orogens are the Kimberley's main sources of mineral wealth. The Halls Creek gold rush (page 68), the iron ore mines of the islands of Yampi Sound and zinc-lead mining at the Cadjebut mine (page 94) are some of the developments so far. The Argyle Diamond Mine (page 97) south of Kununurra in the east Kimberley has been the most dramatic development of mineral resources in recent years. The west Kimberley was explored for diamonds in the late 1960s after it was recognised that the volcanic extrusion in the area was of the type associated with diamonds in other countries. That exploration was unsuccessful.

The rocks of the Kimberley Basin may also provide the basis of major future development: in the northern part there are large fields of bauxite (page 95) formed by prolonged tropical weathering of basalts in the area. And, for energy resources, the main prospect is petroleum from along the margin of the Canning Basin (page 94).

A curious feature of the Kimberley is the striking contrast between streams draining to the north and those draining to the east and south.

Northerly streams like the Drysdale and Mitchell are straightforward: they flow towards the sea from high areas in the centre of the Kimberley. Their course is governed by underlying geological features. The Charnley River, for instance, follows the boundary between very resistant sandstone and more easily eroded volcanic rock.

The Prince Regent River is a striking example of a river responding to the dictates of

(Right) Ramparts rising sheer from the sea to a height of 150 m, the rugged cliffs of Cockatoo Island make access to the inland area difficult. The island's high-grade iron ore deposits were discovered in the 1880s but mining didn't commence until 1951.

(Far right) The world's largest diamond mine and the principal source of deep-pink diamonds, Argyle Diamond Mine is geologically unusual in another way, too. Argyle diamonds are found in a volcanic rock called lamproite. Before the Ellendale and Argyle pipes were found in 1976 and 1979 respectively, it was believed that diamonds were only present in the rock known as kimberlite (which takes its name from the city of Kimberley in South Africa). The Argyle discovery has opened new areas of diamond exploration worldwide.

geological imperatives. It flows straight as an arrow for more than 100 km along a great fracture in the King Leopold Sandstone. Its tributaries flow in at clearly defined right angles, for their courses are guided by smaller fractures which intersect the main one.

Where the northerly streams cross from one rock type to another, the downward angle of the stream bed may change abruptly, resulting in a series of cascades. The Mitchell River makes an even more spectacular shift as it plunges in a series of waterfalls over the edge of the Mitchell Plateau.

By comparison, many of the streams draining to the Fitzroy and Ord rivers in the east and south display a remarkable independence of geological controls. The Hann River cuts straight through some of the highest ridges in the region to join the Fitzroy, which itself cuts first through

the sandstones of the King Leopold Ranges and then the limestone ranges at Geikie Gorge.

The Ord River, too, cuts through major ranges, notably the Carr Boyd and Dixon ranges. The Margaret River slices through a major topographic barrier, the King Leopold Ranges, even though there appears to be a much easier pathway across lower ground around the edge of the ranges. In fact, of the streams draining this eastern side of the Kimberley, only the Chamberlain River shows strong geological guidance: it flows straight across the outcrop of soft shales exposed beneath the upturned edge of the King Leopold Sandstone of the Durack Range.

Why do the rivers of the south and east shun the easy route? In many cases, the answer is that their courses were established when the features visible today were buried under masses of sediment washed down from the main Kimberley block into the Canning Basin. The ancient forerunners of rivers like the Lennard and Fitzroy had an unimpeded passage across the sheets of sediment sloping gently to the southern lowlands. When the rivers cut down to expose the rocks which are the hills of today they had the time to carve through them as they were slowly exposed, so maintaining their courses. This is how the spectacular gorges of Geikie and Windjana were created.

The creation of river valleys through the high barriers of the Carr Boyd and King Leopold ranges was a variation on this. The ancient rivers flowed across broad plains. These plains were then slowly uplifted. The rivers still cut across the rising landscape but as they cut through the strata of different hardnesses, they stripped away soft rocks and left harder ones standing as ridges.

The most striking feature of the Kimberley

Like a coral reef after someone has pulled the plug ... That's a fair description of the scenery at Geikie Gorge. Kimberley limestone ranges such as the one bisected by the Fitzroy River at Geikie Gorge are among the best examples of fossil reefs in the world. Cyanobacteria and other now-extinct lime-secreting organisms were the reef builders – not corals. The white discolouration marks the flood level of the river in the annual wet season.

is the shape of its mountains, a result of the incredible time span in which the basic characteristics of limestone and sandstone were left undisturbed to be shaped by erosion and weathering.

Limestone is very strong mechanically but chemically weak. Because of its mechanical strength it is able to stand in vertical or even overhanging faces but it is readily dissolved by the very weak organic acids formed by the mixing of rainwater with decaying vegetation. The result is

Derby stands on a low, flat peninsula jutting out into the mudflats of King Sound. The highest point in town is only 20 m above sea-level and the demarcation line between permanent vegetation and tidal marshes occurs at an elevation of 6 m or less. King Sound (roughly 150 km by 55 km) is the mouth of the Fitzroy, May and Meda rivers. It has a tidal range of 10 m, a treacherous entrance and extensive shallows.

majestic sheer faces such as those of Geikie and Windjana gorges, and, more common and less spectacular, limestone outcrops fretted with small pits and channels. The dissolving of limestone by groundwater has also produced underground caves and, especially where the roof of a cave has collapsed, steep-sided depressions. These processes are clearly visible at Tunnel Creek where the stream drains a depression on the edge of the Napier Range through a long cave.

However, the limestones of the Kimberley don't have the extensive cave systems and the array of stalactites and stalagmites of places like the Jenolan Caves in NSW or the Margaret River region in the south-west of WA. This is because the climate of the Kimberley, with its long dry season and high rate of evaporation, leaves relatively little water to dissolve the rock.

Sandstone normally exhibits exactly the opposite characteristics to limestone: it is chemically very strong but mechanically weak. The most curious feature of all the Kimberley landforms is that caves are found not only in the chemically susceptible limestones but also in strongly cemented quartz sandstones, among the most chemically resistant of all rocks.

And the caves of the Kimberley are not shallow like those found in sandstone around Sydney; they are deep and extensive. Some occur near the summit of the Cockburn Range, west of Kununurra; however the most outstanding example is the feature known as the "Whalemouth Cave" in the Osmand Range east of Warmun Community. This is 220 m long and 120 m deep and, unfortunately, not accessible to the public. Its name is apt – the exit is 60 m high and 45 m wide!

The reason for this unusual characteristic and resulting landforms is, again, the geological stability of the region. When these sandstones were formed, the pressures within the bedding fused the individual grains of sand together. Groundwater generally can't penetrate this cement but, given time, it can seep along joints and fractures, eventually dissolving the cement and washing away the grains of sand. Gradually, these fractures widen into long, narrow caves. Although the process may have been faster in the distant past when the climate was wetter,

Ranger-in-charge Bob Taylor and visitor Rob Thompson stand deep within a cleft on the western side of the Bungle Bungle massif. Although the ancient sandstone has lost most of the "cement" that originally bonded the rock, individual sand grains are interlocked, giving it the stability to form cliff faces.

As the rock walls of "Cathedral Gorge" glow in the midday sun, the huge cavern at the base of the cliff dwarfs the crouching figure of Rob Thompson examining the clear waters of a pool crowded with tiny frogs. This intriguing composition of red rock, white sand and crystal water is the headwater of a small, unnamed tributary of Piccaninny Creek, the main watercourse of the southern Bungle Bungle Range.

today it is infinitely slow.

The spectacular sandstone formations of the Bungle Bungle Range owe their existence to different causes. In its sandstone, the "cement" between the grains of sand never completely filled the gaps. This allowed rainwater to flow through the rock and eventually wash all the cement away. But even without the bonding, neighbouring interlocking grains support each other. The result is that the rock is mechanically very strong when compressed but very weak when pulled apart. Bungle Bungle Range sandstone can support a weight of 40 megapascals (almost 6000 pounds per square inch) but crumbles away when even lightly struck. This allowed water erosion to carve up the range but what remained was able to stand alone as steep-sided towers, ridges and gorges. The sandstone structures of northern Australia are so reminiscent of the

famous limestone towers of the Guilin region of southern China that geographers first assumed that they, too, were limestone.

One of their most notable features is the surface pattern of horizontal black and orange tiger stripes. Surprisingly, these are less than one centimetre thick – underneath there's white sandstone. The orange is a clay and silica skin and the black is organic, mainly lichens. If it were not for these skins protecting the rock, the range would soon disappear.

As a finishing touch to this spectacular landscape, the Bungle Bungle Range was probably hit by a large meteorite at some time in the distant past. The crater itself has been almost entirely levelled by erosion and today it is only a shallow depression. The most lasting evidence of the impact is that the rock around Piccaninny Gorge has been heat strengthened. Here the

"Tiger-striped beehive mountains" clamoured the first media reports of the Bungle Bungle Range. However, the beauty of the contrasting bands is only skin deep – below lies uniformly white sandstone. The banded skin, less than a centimetre thick and easily broken, is the reason why the Bungle Bungle massif has survived – it inhibits the process of erosion. The orange bands are composed of clay and silica and the black is organic growth, mainly lichens, established wherever the silica skin shatters.

sandstone doesn't fall apart grain by grain but collapses along fractures to form huge cliffs.

The Bungle Bungle Range is not unique; similar structures exist at the Ruined City in Arnhem Land and in the Sahara Desert as well as nearby at Kununurra's Hidden Valley and across the NT border at Keep River National Park. However, it is much larger and is the best example of its kind in the world.

About 100 km north of the Bungle Bungle Range lies the Ragged Range, a complex of conglomerate and sandstone towers. In part, the scenery is like that of the Bungle Bungle Range but without the beautiful symmetry.

At the northern foot of the Ragged Range there is a huge, solitary, enigmatic sand-dune. It stands some 200 km from the desert dunes south of the Kimberley. The sand has undoubtedly been blown from stream beds, but the age of the dune and the conditions under which it formed have yet to be deciphered.

While towers, domes and pillars are characteristic of many of the sandstones in the Ord and Bonaparte basins in the eastern part of the region, the much older sandstones in the Carr Boyd and Cockburn ranges and in the heartland of the Kimberley Basin have been carved into great cliff lines. That's because these sandstones are generally tightly cemented and collapse in great slabs along vertical fractures rather than grain by grain.

Where the sandstone bedding is almost horizontal, as in the Cockburn Range, the landscape is dominated by flat-topped plateaus like those found in the mesa country of the south-west of the United States. Flat-topped mesas bounded by cliffs standing above debris slopes are also common throughout the central part of the Kimberley Basin, especially around the Barnett Range.

Along the northern edge of the Mitchell Plateau there are grand sandstone cliffs dropping sheer to the plains below. In the regions around Halls Creek and the Margaret River, flat-lying sandstones and laterites form caps on low mesas.

Where the rocks have been tilted, the main landforms have cliffs on one side and long slopes on the other. In a particularly picturesque turn of phrase, geographers refer to these as "hogbacks". There are numerous examples of these, especially on the Bandicoot and Carr Boyd ranges. In the more remote Moonlight Valley (on the northern side of the Osmand Range) the tilted glacial beds have produced layer upon layer of resistant outcrops forming a series of cliffs that descend northward like a giant inclined stairway.

But pride of place must be given to the Elgee Cliffs, an array of scarps and tilted benches running northwards for 125 km along the Chamberlain River. The Elgee Cliffs, which are off normal tourist routes (except at their northern extremity), are one of the most outstanding landforms in Australia. They are best seen from an aircraft, and from this perspective, they stretch to the horizon in a single, unbroken escarpment.

The rugged Kimberley landscape has a grandeur second to none. It has been shaped by the erosion of diverse rock masses over enormous spans of time. The geological time scale of the Kimberley reduces over 40,000 years of human occupancy to a scant moment.

The stamp of ancient times is still clearly evident throughout the Kimberley, in direct contrast to the rapid changes typical of more mobile parts of the Earth's surface. The slower tempo of change has not only produced its own unique landscape, it has resulted in formations which challenge geographers' long-held theories of how the world's landscapes were formed.

Towering over the plains of the Pentecost River, the cliff line of the Cockburn Range resembles the walls of a fort. These ramparts are made of strongly cemented sandstone lying in flat, horizontal beds that break apart as blocks to produce vertical cliff faces dropping to steep scree slopes below.

Any close examination of the Kimberley coast fills one with awe at the seafaring skills exhibited by the early mariners skirting these shores. Reefs, shoals and archipelagos guard the mainland and there are huge tides and savage rips at the mouths of rivers and bays. There is also the threat of cyclones, which in the past claimed many vessels. Even today, with infinitely superior instruments, sailing the Kimberley coast is not a journey to be undertaken lightly.

The continental shelf is very wide along this part of Australia's coastline. Around most of the Australian coast, the shelf is consistently about 100 fathoms (approximately 180 metres) deep before dropping steeply away to the ocean floor; on the Kimberley coast, the shelf extends far below 100 fathoms. Steep-sided, partly drowned river valleys (such as the spectacular lower reaches of the Prince Regent River) line the coast and what were once inland hills are now a maze of offshore islands.

Huge differences in the levels of the low and high tides also create a range of shipping problems. In the case of the early ports and jetties, tidal variations of up to 11 m made it essential to arrive at high tide. Today, luggers can come into Broome's old jetty only at the top of the tide and are left sitting on the mud as the tide ebbs. During spring tides (the lowest), the relocated Broome and Wyndham wharves now have about 9 m of water alongside at low water and at least 5 m depth in the approach channels. At Derby both the now-disused wharf and the approach channel are dry in the spring tides.

The tidal range of the Kimberley coast has tempted some far-seeing scientists into experiments in harnessing the tide as a power source. So far, remoteness and construction costs have beaten them. **DMcG**.

Chaotic coast: (Top left) tidal inflow drapes a curtain of water over one of the myriad reefs surrounding Sunday Island at the mouth of King Sound. (Centre left) The Buccaneer Archipelago north of King Sound is characterised by a scattering of islands, peninsulas and waterways. The Kimberley's reefs, shallows and huge tides limit the operations of modern deep-hulled vessels such as the one high and dry near Entrance Point at Broome. Until it ceased operating in 1989, the Kimberley Explorer (below left) was the only cruise vessel regularly plying Kimberley waters.

"Of Droughts and Flooding Rains"

"Weather balloons are filled with hydrogen and make a hell of a mess if they explode," says Andrew Duncan, meteorological officer in Halls Creek. "Static electricity is the principal hazard." After a balloon is launched, the observer climbs into the device alongside the launch site and tracks the balloon on radar, recording wind direction, temperature and humidity data. Balloons expand as external air pressure decreases – most burst below an altitude of 26,000 m.

I was leaning against my four-wheel-drive in Wyndham when the weather report came on the car radio. It was April and the regional forecast for the Kimberley, as usual, was "scattered showers". There wasn't a cloud in the sky and none was to appear during the day. A truck driver standing nearby mirrored my thoughts: "That was a lot of use, wasn't it?" he declared. "A piece of land much larger than England and it's covered in one sentence. Won't rain here but they might catch a bit more over in Broome."

It is understandable that the news broadcasters dismiss the Kimberley in a single sentence: the whole area supports fewer people than a regional town elsewhere. Looking at the Kimberley on the map, one tends to think of this remote, empty region as one homogeneous region but it isn't.

The title of this chapter comes from a line in Dorothea Mackellar's poem *My Country*. It is certainly apt for the Kimberley. There are two general cate-

gories of Kimberley climate. Like the NT north of Katherine, the area within a band running along the coast from the mouth of King Sound to a point north of Wyndham has a "hot, moist climate with a marked dry season in winter". The rest of the Kimberley is categorised as having a "dry, hot climate where winter is drier than summer".

As the map on page 32 indicates, there are wide-ranging differences in rainfall throughout the Kimberley. By far the highest rainfall is in the area around the Mitchell Plateau and the lowest is, not surprisingly, along the fringes of the Great Sandy Desert. Throughout the Kimberley, the monsoonal rains of the tropics are vital: they may leave stations and communities isolated for months on end but they provide the fodder and stored water to see them through the seven or eight dry months. However, in some years the "wet season" provides very little rain and stock must be sold off or they could die.

The sight of cracked, parched earth in dry watercourses is common late in the dry season. In the feast-or-famine climate of the Kimberley, soil loss during floods is extensive. By 1967, before a regeneration program began, it was estimated that over-grazing, which depleted protective grasses, resulted in an average of 29 million tonnes of soil being lost down the Ord River each year.

Although the temperatures throughout the Kimberley conform to the hot summer/cool winter pattern, there are significant variations between towns. Derby and Broome don't experience the top temperatures of Wyndham or Kununurra but they generally have higher humidity and don't cool off as much overnight. Halls Creek, the Kimberley township that lies

because of the weather.

Mayaru (February–March): the weather is better and food crops still growing.

Bandemanya (April): crops maturing and much more food available.

Goloruru (late April): the trade winds begin.

Yirma (May–August): the cold, dry time. A rich time when roots, fruit and seeds are abundant

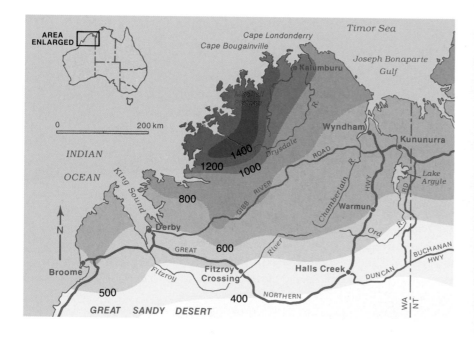

(Above) Average annual rainfall (in millimetres) varies greatly across the Kimberley region.

farthest inland, has less rain and less humidity, as well as generally cooler nights, than the others.

Unlike the broad division of seasons into "Wet" and "Dry", the distinctions developed by Aborigines are much finer. One dialect of the Wunambal group lists seven seasons:

Wundju (January–February): the wet season. Plants are scarce and animals hard to hunt and the grass can be burnt off to herd kangaroos towards hunters. The south-west winds begin. Enough food can be stored to allow gatherings of Aboriginal groups.

Yuwala (September–November): hot and dry. Rivers are drying up and most root crops have been gathered.

Jaward (November–December): the build-up to the wet season with thunder and lightning. Some fruits ripen, replacing the last root crops.

Like other rural areas, the Kimberley is dominated by the seasons. The rain that closes roads often puts airstrips out of action too, so people don't get around much in the Wet (from November/December to March/April). Station work almost ceases and many Aboriginal workers take part in gatherings and ceremonies at this time.

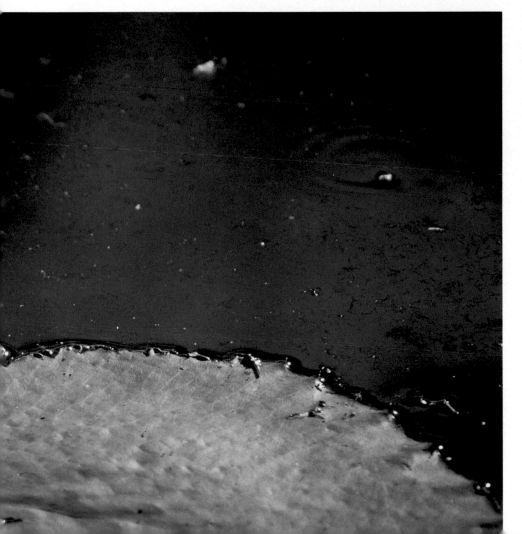

(*Left*) *Looming over an isolated beach north of Bigge Island, an afternoon thunderstorm develops rapidly. The monsoon, or wet season, is a time of spectacularly savage tropical storms.*

(*Centre*) *Life-giving water: the permanent waterholes and billabongs of the Kimberley, such as this one north of Kununurra, are home to an incredibly wide variety of plant and animal life. In 1975, an expedition into the little-explored Drysdale River National Park recorded some 600 plant and 2500 animal species.*

The tourist season starts about April and continues until the humidity and heat become too uncomfortable. This dry season is also a busy time for the rural industries. Towards the end of the year there's tension in the air as large thunderclouds develop each afternoon only to dissipate overnight without rain. One employer told me: "Every staff complaint I've ever received came in the weeks before the Wet." With a cloudburst, the monsoon season arrives. How much rain falls to replenish the parched land sets the pattern of Kimberley life for the next 12 months. **DMcG.**

C y c l o n e s

Engine of destruction: a satellite image of Tropical Cyclone Elsie in February 1987. Elsie started as a low-pressure system in the NT, then headed west to cross the Kimberley coast near Kuri Bay. Once off the coast, Elsie deepened rapidly to become a cyclone. It then recrossed the coast at Mandora station south of the Kimberley, destroying the homestead and drowning all the station's working horses. Elsie then lost strength and became a low-pressure system again, dissipating in the desert south-east of Mt Newman.

Cyclones, those irresistible forces of destruction against which we are powerless, exert a fascination which draws us in just as objects are drawn into the eye of the maelstrom. For anyone living outside the cyclone belt, there is a shiver in contemplating what it's like facing the mightiest engines nature produces. But for those who live there, a cyclone is just a random and dangerous fact of nature.

The Kimberley coast is a cyclone area – a cyclone may arrive at any time between November and April. A beer salesman in Halls Creek told me: "Cyclones are great business for me. When the warning goes out, everyone just puts up the shutters, stocks up on beer and has a few drinks until the danger is all over."

A tropical cyclone is a body of very strong winds rotating around an "eye" of extremely low pressure. Australian cyclones rotate clockwise while those of the Northern Hemisphere (where they are generally known as typhoons or hurricanes) spin anti-clockwise. A cyclone is likely to have a diameter of over 320 km and, near the eye, wind gusts may reach over 300 km/h. These winds have driven stones 15 cm into tree trunks!

Although the part of the Western Australian coast most prone to cyclones is around Port Hedland, the Kimberley near Broome has seen its share. In the days before cyclone warnings, they often resulted in high loss of life. A cyclone which struck the pearling fleet at Eighty Mile Beach in April 1887 was first reported to have left 30 vessels and 500 men missing although the final count of lives lost was 140. Only nine years earlier, in March

1878, a cyclone had destroyed two ships loading guano at Browse Island with the loss of 22 lives.

The township of Broome was worst hit by the cyclone of November 1910. Many buildings were destroyed and the pearling fleet, which was caught on the way to shelter, lost 26 vessels and about 30 men. In late March 1935, the pearling fleet (already hard hit by the Depression and low prices for mother-of-pearl) was at sea when it was struck by a particularly vicious cyclone: 21 of its 52 vessels were sunk and more than 140 men died.

Today, using satellite cloud photographs and radar, meteorologists normally declare a **cyclone watch** if one looks likely to strike a coastal community in 24 to 48 hours, and a **cyclone warning** if the threat is more immediate – within 24 hours.

To the hapless observer, the first effects of a cyclone are wind, rain and rising seas. At the peak of the cyclone's fury, there are shrieking winds and torrential rain. If the eye of the cyclone (which is usually 50 to 60 km across) passes overhead, the wind stops suddenly and there may even be blue skies. The return of the maelstrom is equally immediate with winds at full strength from the opposite direction for several hours, tailing off over several more.

Even when the cyclone has passed, the threat of danger isn't over – cyclones have been known to double back to strike an area again. Or another cyclone may be building up in the Indian Ocean that will subsequently devastate the coast of north-west Australia.

DMcG.

The Original Inhabitants – then and now

by Kim Akerman

One of the most remarkable highlights of Australian history was the arrival of the first people in Australia. This took place much more than 40,000 years ago and the details of those first Australians have been obscured by the mists of time. But archaeologists have pieced together clues which provide a framework for modern theories.

Our early ancestors were *Homo erectus*, who first stood up in Africa in about 180,000 BP (Before Present). *Homo sapiens* evolved much later – the Aborigines are believed to be descendants of early people who travelled down through the arc of land which is now the Malay Peninsula, Singapore, Java, Bali and Timor. This was at the end of the last Ice Age and sea-levels were much lower than they are today as much of the ocean was bound up in the polar ice-caps. The rise and fall of the oceans resulted in Australia being joined to New Guinea on occasions, but there was never a direct link between Australia and Asia.

There were times when the Kimberley coast was separated from Asia by less than 100 km of sea. Those living across the water would have been able to see smoke from fires started in the Australian bush by lightning, so they were well aware that this land existed. It may seem surprising that humans of perhaps 50,000 years ago had the ability to build vessels and an urge to venture farther; but they did. In fact, these human traits shouldn't be a surprise as these people were not an earlier species: they were humans with the same intellectual potential as ourselves. Professor Rhys Jones considers that their vessels were probably rafts made from bamboo. And it was strictly a one-way trip in these craft: there was no indigenous bamboo in Australia, so once here, the migrants were unable to leave.

(**Left**) Dappled by sunlight through coconut palms, a young Broome cyclist pauses in a suburban street. (**Right**) After a hunting trip on the Kimberley coast the spoils are carried back to camp.

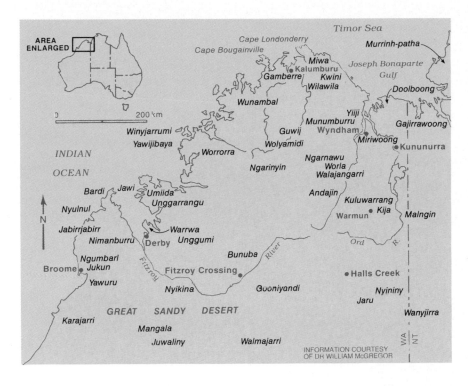

AREA ENLARGED

200 km

Timor Sea

Cape Londonderry
Cape Bougainville

Murrinh-patha

Miwa
Kalumburu
Gamberre   Kwini
Wilawila

Joseph Bonaparte Gulf

Doolboong

Wunambal

Yiiji
Munumburru
Guwij   Wyndham
Wolyamidi

Gajirrawoong

Miriwoong
Kununurra

INDIAN

OCEAN

Winyjarrumi
Yawijibaya

Worrorra

Ngarinyin

Ngarnawu
Worla
Walajangarri

Bardi   Jawi
Umiida
Unggarrangu

Nyulnul

Andajin

Kuluwarrang
Kija
Warmun

Malngin

Jabirrjabirr
Nimanburru   Derby   Warrwa
Unggumi

Ord R.

Ngumbarl
Broome   Jukun

Fitzroy River

Bunuba

Fitzroy Crossing

Halls Creek

Yawuru

Nyikina

Gooniyandi

Nyininy
Jaru

GREAT   SANDY   DESERT

Karajarri

Wanyjirra

WA
NT

Mangala
Juwaliny

Walmajarri

INFORMATION COURTESY OF DR WILLIAM McGREGOR

(Above) The Aboriginal language groups of the Kimberley.

(Left) Spiritually important Wandjina figures, owl like ancestral beings, dominate the work of artists in the north Kimberley. These slate carvings, on sale in Wyndham, were brought down from Kalumburu.

These first settlers almost certainly didn't arrive as a single group. There were probably many landfalls along the coast between the Kimberley and Arnhem Land over thousands of years. The first Australians were skilled mariners: the settlement of Australia was probably the world's first migration accomplished over such wide seas.

Later generations spread throughout Australia and archaeological sites from 40,000 BP have been found in the south of the country – on the Swan River, WA and Lake Mungo in western NSW. The earliest Kimberley sites to have been discovered (at Yampi Sound and Collier Bay) reach back over 24,000 years and on the Ord River, near what is now Lake Argyle, vestiges of human habitation from 21,000 years ago have been discovered and carbon dated.

The first parts of Australia settled are not those that today are yielding the oldest archaeological finds. The reason for this is obvious: today's coastline was only established about 6000 years ago. Settlements would have been at the mouths of the great river systems: the Fitzroy, King Edward, Drysdale, King George, Ord, Victoria and Daly. Coastal lowland settlements of those early days would now be 150 m under the sea and up to 250 km offshore.

The country in which they found themselves appeared very strange. The animals were mainly marsupial and quite unlike the Asian creatures with which they were familiar. Kangaroos 3 m tall, a relative of today's wombat that was the size of a rhinoceros, a leopard-sized marsupial carnivore and goannas up to 6 m long were some of the more bizarre inhabitants. Thylacine and Tasmanian devils also lived in the northern part of the mainland at this time. The diet of the early Australians in the Kimberley appears to have remained consistent (at least over the past 18,000 years) and included shellfish, fish, lizards, rodents, wallabies, possums, bandicoots and goose eggs.

By the time the first European settlers arrived in 1788, the Kimberley population had a highly developed social structure. Of Australia's 29 language groups, at least 15 (and a total of 35 dialects) were in the Kimberley. With typical disdain, early white settlers, who had great difficulty pronouncing Aboriginal words, tended to dismiss the languages as "primitive". In fact, Aboriginal languages have extensive vocabularies and grammar at least as intricate as those of English and other European languages. Like German, Aboriginal languages tend towards single words built up to say what would take an entire phrase

or sentence in English. And, although the lack of an alphabet was taken to mean that there was no written language, whole stories can be symbolised in a single painting.

There is a clear demarcation line between languages of the north and south Kimberley. The line runs from Thangoo station on the coast, along the southern edge of the Canning Basin to Nicholson station, then to Timber Creek in the NT. Languages north of the line predominantly use prefixes and those to the south suffixes. This distinction reflects great differences between the cultures of the north and south Kimberley, particularly in the complex rules governing marriage. Location also played a vital part in determining the pattern of life, which varied greatly. The Wunambal and Worrorra alternated between the coast and rugged inland, travelling along the river valleys, while the Bardi were "saltwater" people, never far from the sea, who exploited the offshore reefs and islands. Along the Fitzroy River, the Nyikina utilised the river and the flood plains, while upstream, the Bunuba lived in the rugged limestone of the Oscar and Napier ranges.

An extensive trade route linked all the groups of the Kimberley and, ultimately, those of adjacent areas and beyond. These trade routes were known as the "Winan" in east Kimberley and "Wunan" in west Kimberley. The "goods" varied from everyday utensils to ceremonial objects or religious songs. Objects were only held for a short time before being passed down the line. So pearl shell from Dampier Land has been found near Adelaide and boomerangs from the desert would be used as ceremonial clap sticks by Wunambal people who didn't make or use boomerangs themselves.

There were fights and battles between groups

(Far left) Etched by brilliant sunlight, Lily Karadata of Kalumburu stands beside one of her bark paintings. Many Aboriginal communities throughout the Kimberley are realising the worth of their traditional art and effectively marketing it in tourist centres.

(Left, top) After the last cattle are in the yards, Norman Rozella of Pentecost Downs station takes a hard-earned break. Long hours in the saddle under the tropical sun ensure Kimberley station work remains one of the hardest jobs on the land.

(Left, below) Playing on instruments donated by Ernie Bridge, State Minister for the Northwest, a band rehearses in the Catholic Hall in Thomas Street, Halls Creek.

but these were to resolve conflicts, not for conquest. Conquest is impossible when no land can be won. Each clan was regarded as holding an area of land in trust and no battle could take that right away. The link between the people, religion and land is not one that can be severed. The Aborigines are bound to the land by ties which extend back to beings who roamed the land (or arrived here from across, or out of, the sea) during the period known as the "Dreaming".

The dislocation of Aborigines as a result of European settlement was great because the land was (and remains) such an integral part of their identity. At first there were skirmishes with explorers and trailblazers but when tne pastoralists and graziers moved in and the Kimberley gold rush occurred, there was strong motivation to completely usurp Aboriginal claims to land in the Kimberley. Aborigines were in demand as pearl shell divers and shepherds but

Posing beneath a mural they created, the artists, workers and organisers of the highly organised Mowanjum Community's art shop take great pride in their artistic endeavours.

both their reluctance to accept pearling work and the fact that some took sheep for food resulted in many being killed. The situation would probably have been even worse had not their labour cost very little. It is impossible to estimate how many were killed (and diseases such as measles, smallpox and flu introduced by immigrants also took a heavy toll) but we can say that many more Aborigines were killed than Europeans. Despite these conflicts, Aboriginal station hands played a vital part in the success of the Kimberley's primary industry.

Several Aboriginal groups died out in the first 100 years of European settlement of the Kimberley. In 1979, it was estimated that six languages and dialects had disappeared and four more were spoken only by the elderly. Many other groups moved away from their traditional lands, often to the towns, where they were forced to adopt a language (mainly

Vibrant colours and intricate design characterise much of Kimberley Aboriginal art. The style dates back to antiquity but the materials may be very modern – this painting is done with acrylic paint on Masonite.

English) in which they could converse with whites and the Aborigines of other groups living there.

Ironically, one of the most disruptive influences on Aboriginal life in the Kimberley was one that was intended to be beneficial. Until 1968, many Aborigines stayed on or near their traditional lands by affiliating with stations in the area. The lease owners could support numerous Aborigines because most were "paid in kind", receiving food and other supplies in lieu of wages. The Pastoral Act came into effect in 1968 ensuring Aboriginal workers received award wages, and this, coupled with a fall in meat prices, led to this source of employment almost ceasing and many Aborigines being forced into towns. Some later formed communities.

Although it's doubtful if she said it, Daisy Bates (who visited the Kimberley in 1900) has long been associated with the phrase "to smooth the dying pillow" because she regarded the Aborigines as a doomed race. It has taken most of this century to remove the destructive force of the rationale behind this epithet. Since the late 1970s there has been a resurgence of Aboriginal self-esteem, noticeably lacking since they were severed from the land.

Towards the end of the 1970s a series of events pushed Kimberley Aboriginal affairs into the national spotlight. In 1977, following the WA State election, accusations were made that the Liberal Party had used unfair means to influence the Aboriginal voters in the Kimberley. The Court of Disputed Returns found that Aborigines had been misadvised by Liberal scrutineers and a new election was called. In this new election, the sitting Liberal Member lost his seat.

Two faces of the Kimberley: Irish-born Daisy Bates (left) maintained her strict dress code even when most inappropriate for the conditions of Beagle Bay and Broome. The evocative expression "to smooth the dying pillow" may not have been used by social worker Daisy Bates but it well mirrors her work with what she considered a doomed race. It became a catchphrase during decades of indifference to Aborigines. The optimistic smile of Andrea Mitchell (right) at Kalumburu is the modern face of the Kimberley. With increasing Aboriginal self-determination throughout the Kimberley, by the time Andrea is an adult there may finally be an equitable balance between black and white in the region.

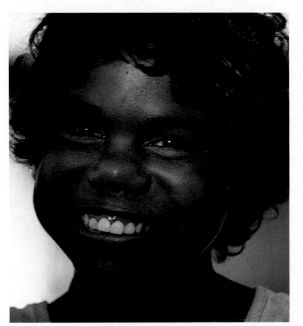

During 1978–80, events on Noonkanbah station increasingly became front-page news around Australia. The first confrontation arose when an oil company's bulldozer driver desecrated a sacred site at Noonkanbah station while the inaugural meeting of the Kimberley Land Council was taking place there. Three years later, the dispute culminated in the oil company being instructed by the Western Australian Government to carry out a test drilling on a sacred site. The drilling rig required a police escort from Perth to Noonkanbah. After drilling, the company reported that no oil was found. But the die was cast: from now on the Aborigines' political voice would continue to be heard.

The Kimberley Land Council became that voice of the Aboriginal people of the Kimberley although, as more Aboriginal corporations have developed the confidence to be self-reliant, it is no longer the sole representative. Further, many corporations are tackling the problems they see within their communities and resolving them.

Australia is coming to realise the worth of the Aboriginal contribution to the nation: the understanding of the environment, the rich cultural traditions and the great merits of Aboriginal art.

The Kimberley, with a population which is about 40 per cent Aboriginal, is set to play an increasingly important part in developing a long overdue understanding of the first Australians.

Joe Edgar, of Goolara-booloo Aboriginal Arts and Crafts Centre in Broome, displays a decorated wooden shield as an example of the high standard of merchandise in the store. "A few collectors seem prepared to pay anything for some items but we endeavour to keep prices moderate and realistic," he says.

The most famous figures in Kimberley paintings are the Wandjina, those eerie faces which have an other-worldly air about them. However, they represent only one form of Kimberley painting: the region embraces five artistic zones as shown in the map opposite.

Zone 1 (A), which takes in a large part of the western and central Kimberley, is the centre of Wandjina art. Kimberley Dynamic figures (also known as Bradshaw figures after the Australian pastoralist and explorer who first reported their discovery in an illustrated paper to the Royal Geographical Society) are found here too. The fine fluid lines which characterise Kimberley Dynamic art were drawn by birds using their beaks, say the Aboriginal peoples whose territory this is. Motifs include humans, fish, reptiles, marsupials and birds.

Zone 1 (B) at the top of the Kimberley has few Wandjina but some of the most spectacular Kimberley Dynamic figures.

Zone 2 includes the Ord Basin and extends into the Victoria River Basin. There are rock paintings in solid colours outlined with fine dots, usually of white ochre. Motifs include fish, reptiles, birds, marsupials, vegetable foods and humans.

Zone 3 extends far beyond the Kimberley to take in much of the west coast. In the Kimberley section, pearl shell was skilfully engraved, as were wooden artefacts. Motifs include parallel meander, interlocking key and herringbone designs as shown in the photograph on the next page. More recently, naturalistic motifs occur – including scenes of contact with Europeans.

Zone 4 covers the basins of the Fitzroy, Mary and Margaret rivers. It is an area rich in rock art and is a mixture of the central Kimberley, Ord and western desert traditions. Simple engravings depicting animal tracks frequently occur but there is also the "knight in armour" of Sturt Creek as an example of a complex work (see the photograph on following page).

So far, the Dynamic figures of the Kimberley can't be dated but they are very old and certainly predate the Wandjina. They also show a level of extraordinary sophistication only matched in Australia by the Dynamic figures of Arnhem Land. The Worrorra, Wunambal and Ngarinyin are the people of the areas in which Kimberley Dynamic paintings exist. Unlike other rock paintings, these were not retouched by later artists.

The Wandjina paintings are believed to have been done by the great creator beings that remain as the paintings or in trees and landforms. Mortals can draw spiritual sustenance from them and senior clansmen can reaffirm the continuity of human life by regularly retouching the paintings (an expression of ancestral bond). If the retouching is done at the appropriate season, it activates the dormant powers of being that maintain the natural cycles of the cosmos.

An event that aroused considerable controversy in the Kimberley in recent years was the retouching or repainting of Wandjina sites between the Napier Range and Drysdale River station. The retouching was carried out by young Aborigines, under the instruction of elders, with the help of a grant under the Commonwealth Employment Program (CEP). Opponents claim that paintings of great artistic merit have been ruined by hack artistry and the materials used are wrong. However, supporters argue that repainting is standard procedure among Kimberley Aborigines, who regard art as part of life and not something for a museum. Scientists were later able to show that only traditional materials were used, although modern materials have been used elsewhere for retouching rock art, such as in Kakadu.

There has been innovation within the artistic styles of the Kimberley in recent years. For example, in the east Kimberley there has been a shift towards portraying the country – in both plan and profile – whereas previously Kimberley paintings (unlike those from other areas) depicted beings and objects rather than places. However, unlike the highly schematised portrayals of landscapes common in the desert country and east and central Arnhem Land, the Kimberley representations are characteristically uncluttered. **KA**.

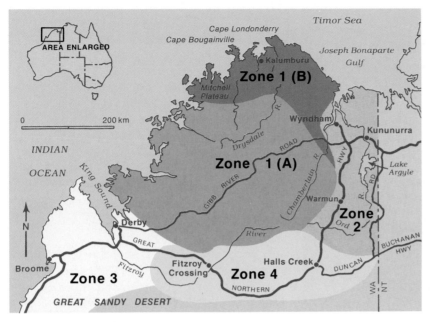

Kimberley art zones.

Kimberley Dynamic (Bradshaw) figures at the King Edward River.

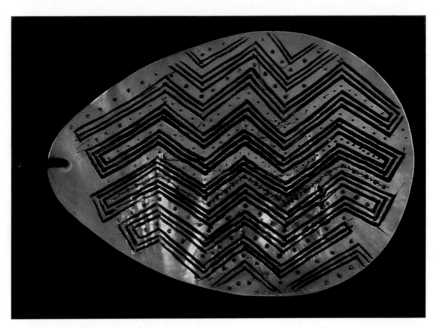

Carving on pearl shell from the west coast.

The "knight in armour" of Sturt Creek.

At Cunningham Point, north-west of Derby, the first mission in the Kimberley was established in 1885 by Father Duncan McNab, a Catholic priest from Scotland. However, the residents had already been victims of "black-birding" raids so it's not surprising that Father McNab had little success in convincing them of the benefits of white religion. In 1887, the mission burnt down, McNab fell ill and the venture was abandoned.

Three years later, Bishop Matthew Gibney of Perth (McNab's supervisor) enlisted the help of several French Trappist monks to establish a mission at Beagle Bay and later to build a branch at Disaster Bay in 1896. Despite the combined efforts of Bishop Gibney, journalist/researcher Daisy Bates, the monks who remained and the local Aborigines, the mission fell into disrepair and passed to the Pallotine Pious Society of Missions in 1901.

While Beagle Bay Mission aimed at assisting Aborigines already affected by the impact of European settlement, new missions started to take Christianity to the others. These included Forrest River (Oombulgurri), Pago (Kalumburu) and Port George IV (Kunmunya).

A government land grant to the Church of England led to the setting up of an Anglican mission at Forrest River in 1897. However, local Aborigines resisted strongly and the Church pulled out in 1898.

It tried again in 1913, with staff brought in from Central Africa, living in a fortified compound on the old site, and appeared doomed to fail again until experienced Australian staff were brought in. Even so, the authoritarian

regime never achieved great success.

Sydney Hadley, a hard-bitten pearler and beachcomber who "got religion" in 1897, established a mission on Sunday Island (in the mouth of King Sound) with the help of two Aborigines from the Forrest River Mission. He did little to interfere with the traditional customs of the Aborigines. However, his unorthodox methods of spreading the gospel, his lack of church affiliation and, perhaps most of all, his overt sexual relationships with Aboriginal women made it difficult for Hadley to muster support for Sunday Island. When the Australian Aborigines Mission took over Sunday Island in 1922, it adopted a much more traditional approach and many Aborigines left for the mainland. Twelve years later the mission followed them, to a site near Cockatoo Island, but this proved unsatisfactory and it moved back to the island in 1937.

In 1908, the New Norcia Benedictines of the Roman Catholic Church of Australia leased land near the top of the Kimberley at a place called Pago and established the Drysdale River Mission. Despite initial animosity and an Aboriginal attack in 1910, the Benedictines persevered, acquiring more land and opening a road to Kalumburu from the Gibb River–Wyndham Road in 1932. The American "Truscott" air base was built nearby during World War II but not before the mission was bombed by Japanese aircraft. The wrecks of several US and British aircraft can still be seen near the runway at Kalumburu. The mission's monastery is still there and its market gardens flourish.

The first Presbyterian mission in the Kimberley was established in 1912 on a lugger moored in Port George IV. It was under the direction of Robert and Frances Wilson who later built a house at the port. However, after three years they had determined that the site was unsuitable and the whole mission moved to Kunmunya. There the fortunes of the mission soared and dipped depending on the kindness or severity of the seasons. However, by the end of the 1940s the vitality of Kunmunya was so badly eroded that the Worrorra Aborigines agreed to accompany the Presbyterians to a new site. They moved to a new mission station at Wotjulum. In 1956 there was another shift, this time to Mowanjum near Derby.

Much of the history of the interrelationship between black and white in the Kimberley has been either in the strictly commercial area of the pastoral industry and pearling or in the work of the missions. There is no doubting the good intentions of the mission workers. Despite that, they faced considerable opposition from other Europeans over the years and, more recently, their work has come to be seen as one of the significant factors underlying present Aboriginal problems. **Cathie Clement**.

(Opposite, below) *Kalumburu's orderliness is readily apparent from the community's neat orchards and vegetable gardens.*

(Opposite, left) *After buying a Cessna 183 from a crop-duster with a taste for comic-book heroes, Father Chris Saunders of the Diocese of Broome painted out the first "s" of "sprayers" to make the sign more appropriate for ecclesiastical usage.*

(Opposite, right) *Sacred Heart Church, Beagle Bay.*

(Below) *Detail of the mother-of-pearl decoration inside Sacred Heart Church, Beagle Bay.*

Alexander Forrest (1849–1901), explorer, surveyor and entrepreneur, was the individual most responsible for opening up the Kimberley. His 1880 Journal of Expedition from De Grey to Port Darwin *reported the Nicholson Plains to be "the finest part of Western Australia that I have seen". He estimated that about 25 million acres had been opened up for pastoral and agricultural settlement by his expedition. His words were subsequently used as a prospectus for Kimberley development. Younger brother of Sir John Forrest, the first Premier of WA, Alexander went on to become mayor of Perth and Member for West Kimberley in the WA Legislative Assembly.*

European Explorers

by Cathie Clement

Although Captain James Cook was the first European to explore the east coast of the continent, he certainly didn't discover Australia. Before he first set foot on Australian soil in 1770, there had been a succession of visitors to the north-west corner of the continent for hundreds, perhaps thousands, of years. The first arrivals were the Aborigines (at least 40,000 years before anyone else), and they came to stay, but some scholars consider it possible that Chinese and Arab traders visiting Indonesia also came south and made brief contact with the Kimberley coast in the centuries before the first Europeans landed there.

By the 19th century, Indonesian fishermen were regularly sailing to the Kimberley coast to collect trepang (also known as sea-slugs or sea cucumbers) between January and May each year. They gave the Kimberley the name Kayu Jawa (which means literally "wood of Java"). Most of their activities took place south-west of Cape Londonderry (near Kalumburu). Because trepang must be boiled and dried before it is transported, the fishermen had to establish shore camps near fresh water, so they inevitably came in contact with Aborigines. Such early liaisons may account for the "light-skinned Aborigines" reported in 1838 by Alexander Usborne, master of HMS *Beagle*, and by George Grey.

The European credited with the first definite contact with the coast of what is now Western Australia is the Dutch captain Dirk Hartog, who arrived in 1616. The first recorded exploration of the Kimberley coast was in 1644 by another Dutchman, Abel Janszoon Tasman (after whom Tasmania, which he also visited, is named).

Tasman's visit is not well documented. Journals recording his voyage, which he undertook on behalf of the Dutch East India Company, have disappeared and only scanty details survive elsewhere. Our main record of Tasman's remarkable achievement is a chart based on

A reproduction of the compass rose used by Captain James Cook RN is the symbol of the Australian Geographic Society. It's a suitable emblem for the Kimberley, too – settlers came to this region from all points of the compass. They first arrived from the north many thousands of years ago; much later, white Australians came with sheep from the south – settling first on the Kimberley's west coast – then later with cattle from the east.

his work in mapping the coast from Cape York to North West Cape. It was this chart that named the land "Compagnis Nieu Nederland" (later generally adopted as "New Holland") and gave us many of the Dutch place names along the coast of Northern Australia.

We do know that 25 men from the three ships under his command landed on the Kimberley coast (probably to the north of Broome) and were given an apparently hostile reception from Aborigines there who were eventually frightened off by a volley of gunfire.

It was the Englishman William Dampier whose two visits to the Kimberley coast are best recorded, and his is the best known of the first European contact with what came to be called Australia. On his first visit in 1688 he was aboard the *Cygnet*, a one-time privateering vessel, looking for new trade routes and opportunities.

Although Dampier had been a privateer, his colourful and much-publicised reputation as a buccaneer is unproven, and was not applicable to the *Cygnet* voyage in any case.

The *Cygnet* was beached for careening and repairs probably north of what is now Cygnet Bay. The crew, who needed food and drinking water, approached some Aborigines seeking assistance but they fled. However, by Dampier's account, the Aborigines were friendly enough once they had conquered their initial fear. They donned cast-off clothes and ate the European food offered to them but declined to work for the mariners.

Dampier's description of the Aborigines as "the miserablest people in the world" is well known. He was less than flattering about the land, too: "A dry sandy soil, destitute of water except you make wells." However, it should be noted that this was in summer, near King Sound and during the Wet when the heat and insects (particularly bush flies) are at their worst. Dampier's impressions may have been different if he had arrived elsewhere on the coast in the infinitely more comfortable conditions of the dry season.

Dampier's major achievement was as a comprehensive (and colourful) diarist. He was the first Englishman to write about Australia. After his return to England he published *A New Voyage Round the World* in 1697, which was an instant success and made him famous. His next nautical appointment was as a captain in the Royal Navy in command of the 290-ton, 12-gun, HMS *Roebuck*. His job was to explore the coast of New Holland. He sighted the coast in August 1699 and entered Shark Bay before proceeding north. Reaching Lagrange Bay, he went ashore on the universal quest of all early

(Top left) Dressed in their best, Abel Janszoon Tasman (1603-59), his second wife, Jannetie, and his daughter by his first marriage, Claesjen, posed for artist Jacob Gerritz in about 1637. In two remarkable voyages, Tasman discovered New Zealand and Tasmania in 1642, then charted the coast of northern Australia in 1644. However, he failed to find the treasures of the mythical South Land and his two southern voyages disappointed Dutch authorities in Batavia (now Jakarta), where the Tasman family lived for many years. Tasman's voyages set the stage for Dampier's exploration of the north coast and Cook's journeys through the western Pacific.

mariners for fresh water.

This time, Dampier's contact with Kimberley Aborigines was less satisfactory than his first encounter. After a skirmish that left casualties on both sides, he obtained some brackish water from a well near the beach. He sailed the *Roebuck* for Timor and later investigated the coast of New Guinea. Dampier's exploits are commemorated by placenames in the Kimberley like Roebuck Bay, Cygnet Bay, the Buccaneer Archipelago, Dampier Land and, in the Pilbara, by the Dampier Archipelago. Most of these names were given by Phillip Parker King many years later. Dampier didn't name anything on his voyage or, if he did, the names did not survive.

However, on both voyages, Dampier's observation, collection of specimens and recording of detail were excellent. In 1699 he noted the presence of pearl shell on the Kimberley coast, little realising that this shell would give rise to a town that would become a centre of the world's pearling industry.

In 1772, the French Lieutenant François Alesne de St Allouarn, in command of the *Gros Ventre,* skirted the Kimberley coast but added little to European knowledge of the continent. Nor did Nicolas Baudin in 1801: this French skipper passed by so far out to sea and at such speed that the scientists who had come with him to study the plants and animals of the continent complained that they couldn't do their job. However, the Baudin expedition added to the great number of French names that dot the coast of Australia from Joseph Bonaparte Gulf in the Kimberley to Cape Rabelais in South Australia.

Phillip Parker King's surveys between 1818 and 1822 included the Kimberley coast. King's surveys were aimed at charting that part of the Australian coast not covered by Matthew

Like this portrait by an unknown artist, lifelong adventurer William Dampier (1651-1715) was a shadowy, romantic figure. His life, much of which is still obscure, was surrounded by controversy but some facts shine through. In 1688, he was the first Englishman to describe Australia – he was not impressed. His first view of the continent was of the Kimberley coast near the Buccaneer Archipelago while he was a crew member of the one-time privateering vessel Cygnet. *He returned to the Kimberley in 1699 in command of HMS* Roebuck.

Phillip Parker King was one of the greatest of Australia's early nautical surveyors. The son of NSW Governor, Philip Gidley King, the younger King was born on Norfolk Island in 1791 and died in North Sydney in 1856. Much of his work was carried out in a series of voyages along the Kimberley coast. He was also the first Australian-born rear-admiral in the British navy. King's early voyages along the north-west coast (from 1818) were in the 84-ton cutter Mermaid; *his last voyage to the Kimberley in 1821–22 was in the 170-ton* Bathurst.

Flinders (that is, the area from Cape Leeuwin, WA north to Arnhem Land). While examining the north-western coast between the Gulf of Carpentaria and North West Cape, King hoped to find a major river flowing from the interior of the continent.

During the four dry seasons King spent working on the Kimberley coast (exploration was only possible during the dry season), he discovered Cambridge Gulf (the mouth of the Ord River) and examined the outer reaches of the sound which now bears his name (and is the mouth of the Kimberley's other major river, the Fitzroy). At Port Nelson he found water was plentiful one season but non-existent the next. In contrast, the Prince Regent River yielded an abundant and reliable supply, and Hanover Bay and Point Cunningham smaller but more accessible supplies.

This close examination of the coast was not without risk. On more than one occasion the racing tides almost cost King his ship, flinging it towards islands, reefs and rocks. The bay named Disaster stands as a reminder of one close shave. Farther to the east, Encounter Cove marks the scene of conflict between King's party and local Aborigines.

In 1821 at Hanover Bay, while King was undertaking the third leg of his survey, there was a more substantial conflict between his men from the *Bathurst* and Aborigines. It was the need for fresh water that took King there but it was curiosity, not necessity, that induced him to go ashore and parley with the local people. He wasn't as welcome as he thought and men on both sides were hurt. No deaths were recorded.

Towards the end of 1836, British interest in the north-west of Australia intensified to the degree that the Government funded two further

explorations in a single expedition under the overall control of Captain John Clements Wickham. The groups set sail in the *Beagle* on 5 July 1837. The previous year the *Beagle* had returned from South America where the ship's scientist, Charles Darwin, had collected the information that would lead to his theory of the origin of species.

Their instructions were to explore and survey those portions of the Australian coast left uncharted by earlier expeditions. In particular, they were to search with the utmost care for the extensive rivers that King and Dampier believed must empty into the large bays to the west of the Prince Regent River.

While Wickham's party used the *Beagle* to survey the coast, Lieutenant George Grey, whose party was sponsored by the Royal Geographical Society, was to explore the countryside. Landing at the Prince Regent River, he was to follow the coast southwards, towards the Swan River, so that he would inevitably cut across any major rivers flowing westward from the interior.

Grey chartered an extra vessel, the *Lynher*, at Cape Town and sailed directly to Hanover Bay. Wickham, in the *Beagle*, proceeded via the Swan River Colony (established in 1829). A severe attack of dysentery delayed him by six weeks and by the time the *Beagle* reached the Kimberley in January 1838, Grey had established a temporary camp at Hanover Bay and was waiting for the *Lynher* to return from Timor with livestock and tropical plants.

Despite King's clash with the Aborigines, Hanover Bay afforded the easiest known access to fresh water on this coast. It also provided anchorage in which the *Lynher* could wait in comparative safety while Grey explored the

A sturdily built vessel, the British 10-gun brig Beagle *(on right) made a significant contribution to exploration of the Kimberley, and the Australian coast generally, between 1838 and 1843. The crew, under the command of Captain John Wickham, filled in the gaps on the chart left by Phillip Parker King and were the first Europeans to navigate the Fitzroy River, exploring the lower 36 km of the Fitzroy's 618 km length. This painting,* Valparaiso 1834, *was painted by Conrad Martens while he was the artist for Captain Fitz-Roy's scientific survey of South America.*

Sir George Grey (1812–98) had a more distinguished career in his later life than any other early Kimberley explorer. His most significant role in the Kimberley was as the first European to venture inland: despite being wounded in a fight with Aborigines, he led a party up the Glenelg and Sale rivers. Although Grey intended to return to the Kimberley, he went on instead to become Governor of SA, New Zealand (twice), and Cape Colony (later part of South Africa). After a period of retirement in New Zealand, he subsequently became Premier of that country. He then returned to England and was made a member of the Privy Council four years before his death at the age of 86.

surrounding countryside. It was at Hanover Bay that Grey introduced exotic plants and animals – including ponies, sheep, goats, pumpkins, breadfruit, coconuts and cotton – to Australia. These were intended primarily for his own use but also with a view to fostering future colonies in the area.

From time to time, Aborigines engaged the explorers in battle. Grey himself was wounded, which curtailed his exploration and this, with other impediments, prevented any attempt at following the coast south to the Swan River.

In the space of three months, Grey's party penetrated inland as far as the headwaters of the Glenelg and Sale rivers. Although unable to find a major river system, Grey was immensely impressed by the land and the harbours he saw and intended to return to the Kimberley with colonists. (When he arrived home he found he couldn't raise the support necessary to implement his plan.)

Wickham's party was more successful than Grey's in discovering rivers. The *Beagle* reached Roebuck Bay in mid-January and surveyed the coast from there to Port George IV before meeting up with Grey in April. Withstanding swarms of voracious mosquitoes (which inspired their naming of Point Torment), sailors braved the tidal rips of King Sound to discover the Fitzroy River.

Squally weather and the sheer volume of water surging in and out of the mouth of the Fitzroy made the exploration hazardous. Nevertheless, a gig and a whaleboat pushed 36 km up the river. Although pleased with their find, the sailors noted debris in trees seven metres above the water and concluded, correctly, that heavy floods sometimes swept this countryside.

The few Aborigines seen along the banks of the Fitzroy fled in apparent terror at the approach of the boats. Yet, at other places along the shores

of Dampier Land and King Sound, Aborigines met these strangers with great aplomb. Unnerved by the Aborigines' lack of fear, the British occasionally undermined their bravado with a display of shooting. Despite this, some Kimberley Aborigines still remained friendly in their dealings with the sailors.

Subsequent British efforts to establish colonies in northern Australia focused on the NT. It was not until 1853 that the Royal Geographical Society again persuaded the British Government to look favourably upon the Kimberley region and at the question of rivers flowing from the interior.

Examining the Victoria River in 1855, Augustus Charles Gregory, leader of the North Australian Exploring Expedition, noticed that this river's major tributaries came from the west. He took a small party westward along the northern edge of the desert and cut the course of Sturt

The Ord River was among the elusive fresh water sources that European explorers had long sought. Phillip Parker King explored Cambridge Gulf but missed the mouth of the Ord. Augustus Gregory set out hoping to find it but passed too far south. It was left to Alexander Forrest to discover the river and name it in honour of Sir Harry Ord, the Governor of WA.

Creek. In the late summer heat, four men and 11 horses plodded from one waterhole to the next, tracing the creek bed almost 500 km south to Lake Gregory (which was dry at the time). Had they taken a more northerly route into WA, they would probably have found the Ord and solved the riddle of the western rivers.

As it was, pastoral expansion in the south and east of Australia eventually placed such huge demands on the continent's grasslands that, by the late 1870s, European exploration of the Kimberley interior was inescapable. The Western Australian surveyor, Alexander Forrest, took the opportunity to open the last of the continent's un-explored plains for pastoral use, an enterprise in which he and his associates had more than a passing interest.

Forrest arranged for pastoralists in the Pilbara region south of the Kimberley to fit out his party with horses and provisions. He secured funding from the Western Australian Govern-ment partially on the strength of the possibility that his party might find gold, an incentive that no doubt added to his sponsors' enthusiasm for the project.

The expedition sailed from Fremantle to the Pilbara in January 1879, then rode from De Grey River station to the Eighty Mile Beach. Fresh water was as scarce as mosquitoes were plentiful. The need for supplies of drinking water brought Forrest and his companions into contact with Aborigines. Initially, the locals were fearful of the intruders but, as the party drew closer to Beagle Bay, the effect of previous amicable encounters with European mariners made the local people more approachable.

Aborigines along this part of the Western Aus-tralian coast had picked up some English words

In a deck of cards John Wodehouse, 1st Earl of Kimberley (1826–1902), would be represented by diamonds. the town of Kimberley in South Africa and the Kimberley region of Australia were both named in his honour. A liberal statesman, he was Colonial Secretary at the time both settle-ments were being established – one as the world centre of diamond mining, the other with great pastoral potential. Unexpectedly, a century later, Australia's Kimberley was found to have enough diamonds to support the world's largest diamond mine.

Plants found in New Holland.

THE INDIAN SEA

English Miles.

Place this at P. 282

The Tropick of Cancer

20

The Ladrone Islands

I. Guam

THE PHILLIPPINE

Phillippine I.

ISLANDS

I. St John

10

Mindanao

I. Meangis

THE SPICE

The Equator

I. Tidore
I. Gilolo

N. Guinea

Bouton
I. Amboina
I. Banda

ISLANDS

10

Ombo

Timor

HOLLAND

20

USTRALIS

A Map of the
EAST INDIES

30

NITA.

and developed a taste for European food and tobacco from boatmen involved in the guano (phosphate) industry on the Lacepede Islands. Forrest was able to capitalise on this as he made his way across to the lower Fitzroy River and into territory unseen by Europeans.

Persistent efforts to find a way through the King Leopold Ranges cost Forrest dearly in horses and the health of his party. He was finally obliged to abandon this quest and make his way to the Overland Telegraph line in the NT. In doing so he discovered the Margaret and Ord rivers. He estimated the river plains would carry thousands of head of sheep. All told, Forrest claimed to have opened up 25 million acres (10 million ha) for pastoral use.

In the Kimberley, Forrest's party had surprisingly little contact with Aborigines. He recorded some opposition on their part but none that actually resulted in battle. Aboriginal tolerance of his party may have been enhanced by the unusually good season and by the fact that, in general, these explorers did not seek out or directly interfere with the people living there.

Forrest's exploration was directly responsible for opening up the Kimberley to European settlement. The Western Australian Government was keen to have settlers take up the land. To capitalise on the money available from the Victorian gold rush, it touted for settlers at the Melbourne Exhibition of 1880. This boosted interest in the Kimberley among eastern colonial squatters and some sent livestock across the continent to take part in Australia's last major land grab. Right from the moment Forrest's favourable report became public, it was inevitable that the Kimberley was soon to receive its first permanent European settlers.

A map from William Dampier's A New Voyage Around the World *(1697) and (far left) Dampier's drawings of the plants of "New Holland". History has proved correct Dampier's judgement that "New Holland is a very large Tract of Land. It is not yet determined whether it is an Island or a main Continent; but I am certain that it joins neither to Asia, Africa, nor America."*

Patriarch of his extensive and influential family, Michael Patrick Durack (1865–1950) was a son of "Patsy" Durack, the instigator of the Durack cattle drive from Queensland to the Kimberley and the founder of Argyle Downs station. Michael Patrick Durack became the business representative of the family's holdings in the Kimberley and negotiated the first sales of Durack cattle to the Perth market in 1893. From 1917 to 1924 he was the Member for Kimberley in WA's Legislative Assembly.

Early European Settlement
by Cathie Clement

The most remarkable feature of European settlement in the Kimberley is that it is so recent: the region was the last in Australia to receive European immigrants. The earliest continuous white settlement of the Kimberley didn't begin until 1879 and many areas weren't settled until the 1920s or later. This is still within living memory of today's inhabitants. When you talk of European settlement of the Kimberley you are discussing the actions of parents and grandparents. There are some names that crop up time and again, Emanuel, MacDonald and Durack among them. Because of the thread of common experience, the people still on their land often speak of people dead before the turn of the century as though they had just left the room.

Kimberley history isn't written text; indeed, it's hard to come by firm factual information. Instead, it really is the story of those who were here only a short time ago.

Since the first cattle were brought in by Nat Buchanan (and shortly after by the Duracks and MacDonalds) the predominant breed of the Kimberley has been Shorthorn. Shorthorns were originally introduced into NSW from England in 1825.

The initial steps towards setting up the Kimberley pastoral industry were taken long before Alexander Forrest and his party left the first bootprints across the region. Early in 1863, liberal new land laws came into effect in WA. These allowed anyone taking stock north of the Murchison River to occupy land there rent-free for the first four years. Those who first decided to take up this offer in the Kimberley focused their attention on the areas and harbours explored by George Grey in 1838. Despite their best endeavours, none of the ventures proved long lasting.

First off the mark were eight Western Australians led by Kenneth Brown. They sailed in the schooner *Flying Foam* to Doubtful Bay in June 1863, carrying enough stores for four months' exploration and 12 months' occupation, as well as seven horses, 25 sheep and two dogs. Establishing a base on the Glenelg River, which flows into George Water to the south-

west of the Prince Regent River mouth, Brown's party explored the coast and surrounding hinterland. After adverse winds kept the *Flying Foam* out of Roebuck Bay, the party abandoned its northern enterprise. In the following year, another Western Australian Government-sponsored expedition, in the aptly named *New Perseverance*, investigated tales of a gold find at Camden Harbour south-east of Camden Sound. The find turned out to be fictitious but the party

entered Roebuck Bay and set up a depot near Cape Villaret before returning to Fremantle.

By this time, sheep graziers had taken up land in the Pilbara. In November 1864, the Western Australia-based Roebuck Bay Pastoral and Agricultural Association (Limited) made camp at Cape Villaret. The manager, James Harding, with Constable Goldwyer and Police Inspector Panter (colonial police often provided protection for pioneer pastoralists) left to look for grazing

(Far left) Sheep Island, a lonely islet near the early settlement of Camden Harbour, served as the community's graveyard. (Left) Dick Smith reflects on the poignant history of Mary (possibly Emily) Jane Pascoe, who died at Camden Harbour on 4 June 1865, aged 30, soon after giving birth to the settlement's first child. Records suggest the baby died three months later on 11 August 1865. The cause of death was not recorded.

The Early Epic Cattle Drives

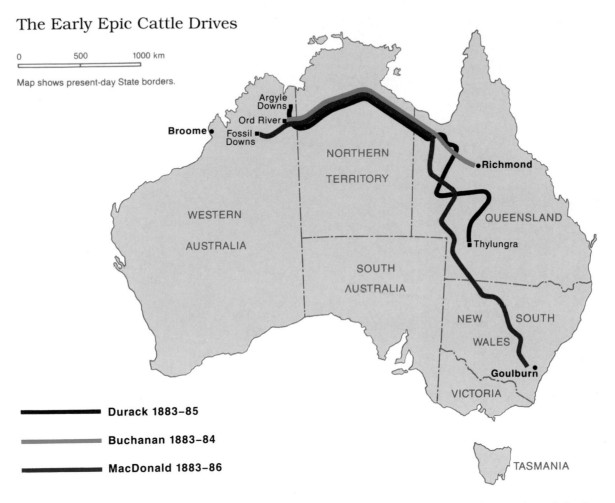

0   500   1000 km

Map shows present-day State borders.

- **Durack 1883–85**
- **Buchanan 1883–84**
- **MacDonald 1883–86**

land towards Lagrange Bay. They were killed by Aborigines after they used guns and dogs to keep the Aborigines away from the waterholes the explorers were occupying. Months later an expedition led by Maitland Brown recovered the remains and dispensed savage retribution.

Meanwhile, another sheep-farming settlement had been formed by Victorians at Camden Harbour but it failed in the face of harsh climatic extremes, poor pasture and Aboriginal resist-ance. Some of the would-be settlers left the Kimberley for the more amenable Pilbara. Although the Roebuck Bay Company considered moving to the Fitzroy River after Alexander McRae rode there from Cape Villaret in May 1866, the move never eventuated; instead, the company pulled out of the Kimberley altogether. Indeed, the sheep industry made little progress until Alexander Forrest's exploration and survey of 1879.

The paths of early epic cattle drives to settle the Kimberley spanned the continent.

Forrest's journey and journals provided the impetus for two groups of Kimberley settlers who had very little in common. Sheep graziers came to the west Kimberley by sea from elsewhere in WA, from NSW and Victoria. They relied heavily on local Aborigines as shepherds (until the late 1880s when fenced paddocks came into use). In the east, pastoralists arrived from Queensland and NSW, some with the cattle they overlanded. These settlers always favoured open-range grazing that required no fences, a style of management that, on the whole, proved more practical in the Kimberley until quite recently, when tick control and breeding programs have required better stock control.

The Western Australian Government printed copies of Forrest's report and used it as a prospectus at its stand at the Melbourne Exhibition in 1880. A ballot for Kimberley land for all interested parties was held by the Government on 1 February 1881. As an attempt to ensure fair land distribution, the ballot was a monumental failure. For example, a cartel of shareholders in the Kimberley Pastoral Company lodged 160 of 448 applications and secured extensive frontages to the Fitzroy and Meda rivers. Liveringa and Meda stations were the result. Forrest hadn't been permitted to participate in the ballot

Returning at the end of an all-day camel ride, tourists cross Cable Beach near Broome. Camels were introduced to the Kimberley during the gold rush of 1886 to bring supplies from Derby. Strangely, some of Australia's first camels arrived in Hobart in 1840, although most were later introduced into the more suitable dry areas of SA. By 1901 there were about 400 "Afghan" cameleers in Australia and one, Adroman Khan, had a string of 25 camels delivering tea, flour and other supplies to Kimberley stations.

The gracious foyer of Fossil Downs homestead, completed by Maxine and Bill MacDonald just after World War II, represented a new age of permanence in the Kimberley after decades of "making do" and "near enough is good enough for the bush". A waterbag from the original MacDonald cattle drive, the world's longest, takes pride of place on the bloodwood staircase. Nearby, award ribbons for cattle cover one wall.

because of his official role as a government surveyor but by 1882 he was a member of the Kimberley Pastoral Company. By 1883 he and his associates held most of the prime land in the west Kimberley. Yet William Marmion, the guiding force behind the most powerful of the region's early land-owning concerns, never even visited the Kimberley.

Some sheep had been rushed into the Kimberley after Forrest's expedition and before the ballot. These reached the Fitzroy River in March 1881. Some went onto the Murray Squatting Company's Yeeda station on the Fitzroy River, while others eventually stocked Balmaningarra station on the Lennard River.

In November 1884, the Emanuel family, which went on to become one of the leading Kimberley families, shipped its first sheep to King Sound. The family diversified into cattle in 1885 and moved to the Fitzroy River the following year, establishing Lower Liveringa, Noonkanbah and Gogo stations.

The colonial government made a big mistake in not insisting that some of the annual rent on the leases be paid in advance. In effect, anyone could secure a large section (even a million acres or more) of the Kimberley for no more than a nominal application fee (of two shillings and

sixpence) and hang on to it in the hope that someone would be prepared to buy the lease before the rent was due. Many parcels of Kimberley land became mere gambling chips held by entrepreneurs who had no interest in stocking the land.

Inevitably, land speculation was rife and this unproductive manipulation greatly slowed pastoral development. In 1883, over 51 million acres of the Kimberley were leased but market forces rationalised that to about 14 million by 1887.

Much of the fascination the Kimberley holds throughout Australia stems from the astounding cattle-droving feats of the eastern colonial over-landers. Three names stand out: MacDonald, Durack and Buchanan.

The man responsible for the establishment of Fossil Downs, a property of just over one million acres (400,000 ha) near Fitzroy Crossing, never saw his dream come true. Donald MacDonald's imagination was fired by the potential of this distant new region after receiving a letter from Alexander Forrest detailing his discoveries. His descendants, who still own Fossil Downs, have retained the letter, but Donald MacDonald was thrown from his horse and killed on the eve of the expedition's departure for the Kimberley. However, his sons followed the venture through.

They left Tuena, near Goulburn, NSW, in March 1883 with 670 head of cattle and 36 draught bullocks. The MacDonalds' herd arrived at Fossil Downs, 5600 km distant, just over three years later. It was the world's longest cattle drive and the bullock wagon that survived the odyssey through to Derby is believed to be the first vehicle to cross the Australian continent. Most recently, Fossil Downs was owned for several decades by Maxine MacDonald (see "Tribute" in

Descendant of the Durack pioneers and chronicler of Kimberley settlement, Dame Mary Durack Miller is best known for Kings in Grass Castles *(1959). She has written or co-authored nine other books and many articles on outback life. The widow of the pioneer aviator, Horrie Miller, she lives in Nedlands, a Perth suburb.*

AUSTRALIAN GEOGRAPHIC Issue nine, p.112) and managed by Annette and John Henwood, her daughter and son-in-law. Sadly, Mrs MacDonald, a true Kimberley pioneer, died soon after the AUSTRALIAN GEOGRAPHIC research team visited Fossil Downs in 1988.

The story of the Duracks is brilliantly told by Dame Mary Durack in *Kings in Grass Castles* and *Sons in the Saddle*. Several waves of Duracks and their stock left Thylungra station on Cooper Creek and other Queensland cattle stations in June, July and August 1883. They all met up along the Thompson River. More than two years later, at the end of the drive, in September 1885, "Long Michael" Durack (as distinct from cousin "Stumpy Michael" Durack, the first to hold a lease over part of what is now known as the Bungle Bungle Range) created an Argyle Downs station landmark when he carved his initials on a tree near the Ord River. The Duracks established Argyle, Dunham River, Ivanhoe and Lissadell stations. In April 1989, Spirit Hill, the only station in the north that was still owned by a Durack – it's just across the NT border from Ivanhoe station – was sold by Reg and Enid Durack.

The last of these early pioneers is a legend of Australian pastoral history. Nat "Paraway" Buchanan was born in Ireland in 1826 and died on his farm near Tamworth, NSW in 1901. He was called "Paraway" after the Aboriginal pronunciation of "far away", his invariable answer when asked where he had come from. He didn't bring his own cattle to the Kimberley; he was droving Osmand and Panton's stock from central Queensland to their leasehold which became Ord River station. Buchanan assumed control of this drive on the Flinders River below Richmond in May 1883 and arrived on the Ord in June 1884.

This pioneer pastoralist, drover and explorer

Nat Buchanan (1826–1901) was the first person to overland cattle into the Kimberley (for Osmand and Panton), arriving at what was to be Ord River station in June 1884. He also pioneered the infamous Murranji Track stock route from Newcastle Waters to the Victoria River.

also opened up the Murranji Track in the Northern Territory in 1886 while taking horses from Queensland to Wave Hill station. Immediately after this, he pushed 1800 head of Wave Hill cattle through unknown country to form a new station on Sturt Creek and started butchering on the Halls Creek diggings. Parts of his route are now followed by the Buchanan Highway.

As in other parts of Australia where gold was found, the gold rush gave Kimberley development an enormous boost. Indeed, the short-lived rush had an impact out of all proportion to the size of the find. Poor communications from this far corner of the continent ensured that many would-be fortune seekers were just arriving when the majority of disillusioned diggers were pulling out.

On 2 September 1872 the Colony of Western Australia offered a reward of £5000 to anyone who discovered a workable goldfield within 300 miles (500 km) of any declared port in the colony. That immediately triggered a lot of interest but the first indication that there was gold in the Kimberley was when a geologist with Alexander Forrest's expedition of 1879 suggested that the source of the Fitzroy River might be gold-bearing. Soon after, Pat Ahern and another man whose name is uncertain rode in from the NT to prospect the area. Neither was seen again.

A better equipped and more fortunate party led by Philip Saunders, a well-known prospector of the time, rode from the Pilbara through the Kimberley to the NT in 1882. Although their expedition was dogged by illness, they turned attention to the east Kimberley by finding traces of gold around the upper Ord River valley. The Western Australian Government became directly involved when it sent Edward Hardman, an Irish geologist, to the Kimberley in 1883 and 1884. He, too, pinpointed the Ord watershed as the most promising area.

Prospectors from all over Australia applied for a similar boon of government-sponsored prospecting but to little avail until, late in 1884, Charles Hall and John Slattery were granted permission to use some government horses not immediately required by surveying parties.

As a general rule, prospectors are not prone to declaring their findings. Although other prospectors were around the area at the same time and may have found gold earlier, Hall and Slattery were the ones who first went public, announcing on 8 August 1885 that they had found 10 ounces (283 grams) of nuggetty gold at Halls Creek on 14 July.

After notifying the Government, they attempted to consolidate their claim on the reward by giving their story to the newspapers. Despite this, they never received the money. The Government argued that neither they nor several other claimants fulfilled a specific condition of the offer that a certain amount of gold must be produced by the resulting field. They probably came undone because there was a duty on gold finds: undoubtedly, a lot of gold left the region undeclared in prospectors' pockets and saddlebags.

However, finder's fee or not, word soon spread on the "bush telegraph" that there was gold in the Kimberley and other prospectors were soon on their way. "Black Pat" Durack and August Lucanus each set up stores at Cambridge Gulf to capitalise on the expected rush; by October they were selling supplies to small parties of diggers. Meanwhile, city newspapers were cautioning that Halls Creek was very isolated and the field had yet to prove its worth. Even so, far more tantalising rumours circu-

lated about the good prospects of the field. By early 1886 about 30 European prospectors were working the area, supported by mates who brought them supplies from the coast. These fields, unlike others in Australia, did not allow Chinese miners.

As more gold came into Derby from the field, gold fever gripped the tiny waterside township and spread throughout Australia and New Zealand. Speculators who had invested heavily in Kimberley land without return saw

potential profits in the rush. The combined efforts of merchants, pastoralists, government spokesmen, land speculators and shipping agents led to a flood of Kimberley news in newspapers around Australia. Voices of caution were drowned in the clamour of the thousands heading for the new El Dorado.

By September 1886, the makeshift camps of more than 2000 prospectors dotted the Halls Creek goldfield. The population was almost entirely male; Aborigines had been driven from

the main field by a savage punitive expedition after a prospector had been killed by an Aborigine in June. Most of the prospectors had to carry dirt long distances to water to wash it or otherwise use the much more uncomfortable and less productive dry-blowing method to find gold. Heat, fever and dysentery, combined with frequent food shortages and a roaring trade in grog, took their toll. Moving daily from one gully to the next, the ranks of diggers were swelled by newcomers determined enough to proceed past the many disillusioned heading out. But many arrivals never made it beyond the canvas towns of Derby and Wyndham after receiving discouraging on-the-spot information. And the wagons and harnesses of those leaving the field sold for a pittance as the owners abandoned them.

Many who were on the point of leaving stayed when one promising new reef was found followed by several more late in the 1886 dry season. None of the finds was substantial. When the rains came in December 1886, there were 800 persevering prospectors in the Kimberley, many looking beyond Halls Creek to areas like Panton River and Mt Dockrell. Continual rumours of new finds kept the hopeful on the move. Only the finders knew how well they really fared; few were prepared to let the Government tax their hard-won finds.

By mid-1887, the European population of the goldfield was around 500, a quarter of what it had been less than 12 months earlier. Prospects looked brighter when heavy reefing machinery was brought in but the field continued to disappoint, never matching the illusion conjured by its promoters. It's estimated that

the field produced a total of about 23,000 ounces (approximately 650 kilograms) of gold by 1896. Eventually, most of the prospectors moved on, some blazing the trail for the rush on Australia's richest goldfield, Coolgardie, in September 1892. Coolgardie produced an impressive 3000 ounces (85 kg) in a single month.

By 1890, only 70 Europeans were still around Halls Creek. In all, the Kimberley may have seen as many as 10,000 arrivals during the gold rush. Of those who stayed, some, like Francis Connor and Denis Doherty, became prominent in Kimberley affairs. It was essentially a storekeeper's rush: the instant infrastructure of police stations, postal services and the telegraph link with Perth (which was operative by April 1889) was its legacy to pastoralists who otherwise would have waited decades for these services.   **CC**

Crumbling mud bricks and a fireplace open to the sky are all that remains of the post office at old Halls Creek, once the centre for a booming gold rush community of 2000. Today it is a ghost town. For practical reasons the townsfolk voted to move to a new site, 14 km away, in 1948. The report of Charles Hall, John Slattery and four others to the Government Resident in Derby of 8 August 1885 started the Halls Creek rush by detailing how "it was at this point that we found payable gold, which we now show you. The weight is about 10 oz. The gold lay in the bed of the creek, quite close to the surface, merely covered by the drift sand". The field was quite small and had produced only about 650 kilograms of gold by 1896. But even then the returns were dwindling, although one mine continued to operate until the 1950s.

Opening Up The Land

Motionless after the last breath of evening breeze, the gaunt skeleton of a windmill is silhouetted by the setting sun. This windmill, which pumps water for the vegetable gardens of Kalumburu, follows an Australian tradition. By the mid-1950s it was estimated that Australia had at least 250,000 water-pumping wind-mills. Australia's geared windmills are based on American patterns but this simple direct-acting windmill is an Australian innovation: each revolution of the blades produces one stroke of the pump.

For its first 40,000 or more years of settlement, the Kimberley was relatively self-contained. Trade routes had been established within the area and there were links with other parts of Australia and with the fishermen of Asia. However, to the white settlers who arrived, the Kimberley was not sufficient in itself: it was the "remote north-west". It has taken 100 years to overcome this isolation. On the way, several Kimberley developments in road and air transport and telecommunications were also milestones in opening up Australia.

The initial surge of development of Kimberley supply routes was aimed at servicing the Halls Creek gold rush of 1886. Camels, bullock and horse drays came from Derby, packhorses (and later, camels) from Wyndham. Later, donkeys and mules supplemented the horses when they proved to be more suitable. Inland mail was originally carried by police (and recipients had to collect it from Halls Creek) before contractors took over and made deliveries en route. In 1889, a six-weekly mail service between Wyndham and Halls Creek was introduced. That was the year after the Adelaide Steamship Company won the contract for a six-weekly mail service between Fremantle and Wyndham.

By 1930, pastoralists from as far inland as Halls Creek were using their own motor trucks and cars to collect stores from the ports. In the early 1950s, the northern part of the longest classified road in Australia, the Great Northern Highway from Perth through Meekatharra to Wyndham, was described as "numerous hazardous creek crossings, marshy sections, patches of heavy sand and rocky outcrops". There was no serviceable road link between Wyndham and Darwin: one was developed later to service the Ord River Scheme. Finally, the opening of the Fitzroy Crossing–Halls Creek tar section, the last

The sealing of a section of road generally doesn't warrant a commemorative plaque, but when part of a road near Halls Creek was finished in September 1986, it was an important event. It meant that Australia's Highway One, which runs virtually the perimeter of Australia, was finally sealed for its entire length. Only a few decades before, the highway had been, in reality, a potholed track with numerous river crossings.

link in an all-sealed Highway One around Australia, in September 1986 gave the Kimberley a road more suitable for the many cars, ore carriers and road trains using it today.

The telegraph line from Roebourne through Roebuck Bay (Broome) to Derby was completed in April 1889. The "goldfields extension" was completed in October 1889, even as the goldfields were dying. After that line was opened it still couldn't be used much in those early days as it frequently failed due to heat, wind and lightning strikes. Also, Kimberley Aborigines discovered that broken insulators made excellent spearheads and that guy wires were equally useful. Another substantial disadvantage was that no telegraph operator came to the goldfields until six months after the telegraph line was completed. The Wyndham Telegraph Station wasn't opened until January 1893.

The townships were the first parts of the Kimberley to come into the Australian telephone network but even their connection lagged well behind just about everywhere else in Australia. Wyndham and Kununurra were the last to join in with a radiotelephone link in 1965. It was partly replaced by a land line in 1967.

Australia's introduction to the age of radio began with the establishment of coastal radio stations, including one in the Kimberley. These were not for entertainment but for ship-to-shore communication. Broome Radio (call sign VIO) started operating in 1913, at least 10 years before the first regular entertainment radio broadcasts began in Australia and 19 years before the ABC was created. Radio VIO still operates today, as an information, weather and safety service for shipping reports, and a radio medical advisory service that links ships with a shore-based medical officer. However, the bulk of the station's work

Lumbering giant of northern Australia, a road train drives through Wyndham carrying cattle to the wharf for shipping to Borneo. In the absence of a railway, road trains are the only means of carrying bulk cargoes in the Kimberley. Bigger than anything else on the roads in Australia, these massive transports are made up of a powerful prime mover and several trailers. They can be encountered on any road in the outback; their width and length call for care on the part of motorists when passing or overtaking.

is in exchanging commercial information between vessels and their agents and owners. Along the treacherous Kimberley coast, VIO is an ever-present reassuring voice.

Although an international cable from Broome to Indonesia ensured that the Kimberley was instrumental in linking Australia to the world from 1889, communications within the region have always been very difficult. Until the 1980s, communication among Kimberley stations and towns and their contact with the outside world was haphazard to say the least. When the pedal radio was developed in the late 1920s, stations could radio messages to the Royal Flying Doctor Service bases and, through them, send messages as telegrams via the postal service. Later, when voice transmission became possible, the RFDS could patch radio calls into the telephone network and Kimberley stations had their first direct contact with the rest of Australia.

Until 1986, the chatter of the RFDS radio was a constant background noise in every Kimberley station and outpost. Outside the scheduled formal

Reaching towards the sky – and across the world – a Telecom microwave tower between Broome and Beagle Bay adds an alien element to the natural landscape. Part of the longest solar-powered telecommunication system in the world, the microwave links have drawn the Kimberley into the wider Australian community. No longer reliant solely on sporadic mail deliveries and static-laden conversations through the Royal Flying Doctor Service radio, people on Kimberley stations and in remote communities can now make telephone connections as easily as their city counterparts.

broadcast times, "galah sessions" allowed a general exchange of information in which every person with a set could participate. There wasn't much privacy but every property felt in touch with others, even when the nearest was many kilometres away.

However, in November 1982 the national telephone system was extended by microwave to Broome and Derby. The Kimberley Microwave System was further extended to Wyndham and Kununurra in September 1983. The final link in the circuit, through to Katherine, NT, was added in 1987. It is the longest solar-powered microwave system in the world. Repeater stations occur every 40 km and every station and community within 50 km of the route is on line. The immediate result of building the system was that about 80 of the 100 RFDS radios in the Kimberley became redundant. The rest were linked in 1988. The galah sessions died out. Although there is now the privacy of the telephone, many miss the close community spirit engendered by the open radio conversations.

Television first came to the Kimberley in 1985 in the form of the ABC. At first it was only available to the towns but the launch of Aussat made ABC television accessible to all who had satellite receivers. The Golden West Network was introduced to Kununurra, Wyndham, Halls Creek, Broome and Derby in 1986 and Fitzroy Crossing in 1988.

Just as Australia was well suited to air travel, the sparsely settled Kimberley has been very receptive to advances in aviation. And as the first sea navigators made landfalls in the Kimberley and NT because these were the closest points to Asia, early aviators' first view of Australia was frequently the Kimberley coast. Indeed, Derby remains the site of a major naviga-

tion aid for commercial jets en route from Singapore to Sydney and Melbourne.

The first airmail service in Australia commenced between Geraldton and Derby in 1921. This was the same year that the company, Western Australian Airways Ltd, owned by Norman Brearley, employed Charles Kingsford Smith as one of its pilots. "Smithy", who had served as a fighter pilot over the Western Front, was later involved in great controversy after a Kimberley flight.

The first crossing of the Pacific, the first non-stop flight across Australia and the first trans-Tasman flight (and return) had all made Kingsford Smith and co-pilot Charles Ulm national celebrities. Their aircraft, the *Southern Cross*, was one of the best known and most loved objects in Australia. So the eyes of the nation were upon them in March 1929 when they took off to fly

Michael Cusack, who, with his wife, Susan, became AUSTRALIAN GEOGRAPHIC's *"Wilderness Couple", makes a call from the telephone at Pantijan station. The telephone's basic setting: a canvas covered lean-to in a paddock near the microwave tower, belies its space-age technology. Several cattle stations have installed computer modem links and facsimile machines.*

Connection of the past: *with the final microwave telephone network links in place in 1989, an important function of the Derby radio station of the Royal Flying Doctor Service became obsolete. The Flying Doctor radio is now almost entirely a lifeline, not a communication line. This has meant a loss of revenue at a time when the operating costs of the service's medical operations continue to rise.*

non-stop from Richmond, NSW, to Wyndham and then on to England. After encountering a storm and running low on fuel, the *Southern Cross* landed on the mudflats at the mouth of the Glenelg River south of Camden Sound. A massive search was launched and the aviators were found 12 days later. They had survived on a diet of mud snails, the small supply of food in the aircraft and weak coffee laced with brandy, a mixture they jokingly named "Coffee Royal". Unfortunately, two old flying friends of Smithy's had died during the search and a rumour spread that the forced landing was a publicity stunt gone wrong. The Prime Minister ordered an inquiry. Although this completely cleared Smith and Ulm, rumours about the "Coffee Royal" affair lingered for years after. Kingsford Smith successfully completed the flight to London in June the same year in 12 days and 18 hours.

In 1931, the speed record from Australia to England was broken twice by aircraft leaving from Wyndham. Both were de Havilland Moths. The first such occasion was when C.W.A. Scott took 10 days, 23 hours, a time soon eclipsed by Jimmy Mollison's flight time of 8 days, 21 hours and 25 minutes. Then, in 1933, Kingsford Smith landed in Wyndham only 7 days, 4 hours and 38 minutes after leaving England.

Initiated as an innovative alternative to long cattle drives along bad tracks, the Air Beef abattoirs were built at Glenroy station in the east Kimberley in 1949. Here, cattle were slaughtered and chilled before being flown to Wyndham for freezing and export to the UK. In 1965, the year after the Beef Road opened, the abattoirs closed. They burnt down the following year. Road trains which carry live cattle along the Gibb River Road to Broome meatworks have replaced the air service.

Development of commercial aviation in the north-west of WA became very much the domain of MacRobertson Miller Aviation (MMA), founded in 1927 by former fighter pilot Horrie Miller with money supplied by chocolate magnate Sir Macpherson Robertson. Its break came when it won the government contract to fly mail between Perth and Daly Waters, NT. In 1949, the company pioneered the air transport of chilled beef from Glenroy station to Wyndham

(Below) A maze of sandbanks, mudflats and mangroves near the Glenelg River was the scene of one of the most harrowing events in the lives of pioneer aviators Charles Kingsford Smith and Charles Ulm. A forced landing left them stranded near here (above) for two weeks in 1929 but both were rescued unhurt. The real tragedy was that two of the search pilots died. Rumours spread that Smithy's "disappearance" was a publicity stunt. The four-man crew was later completely exonerated in a public inquiry into the incident.

On the ground at Derby after a thunderstorm, an Ansett WA aircraft continues a service begun in the pioneering days of Australian aviation. Horrie Miller founded MacRobertson Miller Aviation in South Australia in 1927 with money provided by confectionery magnate Sir Macpherson Robertson. Operations shifted to WA to provide an air service between Perth and Katherine, NT, via the Kimberley. In 1969, MMA became a wholly-owned subsidiary of Ansett Transport Industries.

meatworks. MMA was bought by Ansett Airlines in 1978 and later became Ansett WA, which is still the only airline servicing the Kimberley. Horrie Miller, who was married to Mary Durack Miller (her books are published under her maiden name), died in 1980 and there is a monument to him in Weld Street, Broome.

Aviation continues to play a vital role in the Kimberley. Every station and community has an airstrip and the major regional airports are host to a mixture of Ansett WA aircraft, charter operators (both fixed-wing and helicopter), the Royal Flying Doctor Service, an assortment of mining and pastoral planes and a regular stream of aircraft "just passing through". Although these aircraft are closely monitored by air traffic control in Derby and Kununurra, there's still an element of adventure about flying in the Kimberley – a lot of areas are still uninhabited and there's plenty of "tiger country" where there is nowhere at all safe to land. **DMcG.**

Landing on Lake Kununurra, this Canadian-made Beaver float plane is owned by Alligator Airways, based in Kununurra. Great expanses of the Kimberley have no air-fields and float planes or helicopters are the only easy means of access.

The war in the Pacific was close enough to the Kimberley to make the prospect of enemy action very real. On several properties caches of food were established to be used by resistance forces in the event of a Japanese invasion. Landowners were trained in guerilla warfare and decoding ciphers in preparation for a time when the war would be fought on Australian soil. That never eventuated but the Kimberley was in the front line of aerial attack.

In December 1941, when Japan entered the war, about 500 Japanese were working in Broome's pearling industry. In the wartime hysteria, even those born in Australia of Japanese descent were classed as "undesirable aliens" and sent to Perth to be interned for the duration of the war.

Not all the population flow was outward, however. Broome and Wyndham received thousands of Dutch refugees who had been evacuated ahead of the Japanese advance across Java. An estimated 8000 refugees passed through Broome in the first months of 1942.

The threat of enemy attack on the northwest became real less than three months after Japan had entered the war – Darwin was bombed on 19 February 1942. This was enough warning: nearly all European women and children were evacuated from Broome by boat eight days later. Only Mrs Marjorie "Biddy" Bardwell, the telephone exchange operator, and Sister Catherine Hayes and the children she was taking to Beagle Bay mission remained in Broome alongside the men.

At 9.30 on the morning of Tuesday, 3 March, a formation of nine Mitsubishi Zeros dived out of the sky over Broome and started strafing the 15 flying boats in Roebuck Bay, a collection of Dutch and US navy, RAF, RAAF and Qantas aircraft. Unfortunately, because of a shortage of accommodation in town, most of the passengers and some crews had slept on the aircraft overnight and were on board at the time of the attack. All the aircraft were destroyed but the Zeros avoided firing at the vessels nearby or at the many people lining the shores.

The attackers next turned their attention to the nearby airstrip, where seven large aircraft were standing. A US Liberator managed to get into the air but was shot down over the sea and of the 33 people on board only a single crew member survived. All other aircraft were destroyed on the ground but not before one of the heroes of the day, a Lieutenant "Gus" Winckel, removed a machine-gun from his Royal Netherlands Air Force Lodestar. Resting the gun on his arm (which he burned badly in the process), he is believed to have shot down the Zero that had downed the Liberator. One other Zero also failed to make it back to its base in Timor after being damaged by ground fire.

An estimated 70 people died in the attack on Broome; many of these had only arrived the day before. On the same day there was a Japanese air raid on Wyndham that destroyed one aircraft and a petrol dump. On 20 March, Japanese bombers and fighters returned to Broome. This second attack destroyed one small passenger aircraft and killed a man.

A most curious incident followed the first air raid on Broome. As the attacking Zeros returned home, they crossed paths with a DC3 of KLM's East Indies subsidiary KNILM, piloted out of Java by Captain Ivan Smirnoff. After the aircraft received some direct hits (including four which wounded him), Captain Smirnoff made an emergency landing on a deserted beach between Broome and Beagle Bay. With remarkable skill, as he landed he slewed the aircraft into the surf to extinguish a fire in the port engine.

Eventually, the captain and the other survivors were rescued but a package about the size of a cigar box (addressed to the Commonwealth Bank, Melbourne), which had been given to him just before take-off, was missing. Only later in Melbourne did Captain Smirnoff learn that the parcel contained diamonds worth an estimated £300,000 at 1942 prices (about $10 million today).

It was later established that a 45-year-old beachcomber and lugger captain by the name of Jack Palmer found the parcel of diamonds in the abandoned hulk of the aircraft just a few weeks after the crash. Over the next six weeks he gave some of the diamonds to a couple of friends operating a lugger and generously distributed lots more to numerous Aboriginal and European friends living along the coast.

Palmer and his two lugger-operating friends were variously charged with stealing and receiving. All three were acquitted because the evidence was "unsettled". Diamonds with a total value of about £21,000 were recovered (the best of which Jack had kept in a pair of salt and pepper shakers) but most of the gems (including the most valuable ones) were never accounted for. "Diamond" Jack Palmer continued to live in Broome and always seemed to have plenty of money, although he worked only occasionally. He died in September 1958 at the age of 67. A bag containing £1000 disappeared from his hospital bedside on the night he died. What happened to it and the more substantial fortune in diamonds remains a mystery. **DMcG**.

A World War II aircraft wreck in the bush at the side of Kalumburu airfield.

One of the more unusual plans in the history of the Kimberley was the proposal, before and during World War II, to settle a large number of Jewish refugees from Europe there.

The scheme had its roots in the formation of the Freeland League for Jewish Territorial Colonisation in London in 1935. This body aimed to set up self-supporting agricultural communities of European Jews outside Europe. In January 1938, a London-based Australian journalist, S.H. Chomley, wrote a series of articles promoting the Kimberley as a likely site. He argued that one benefit for Australia would be the greater protection such settlement would give against possible invasion from the north.

Back in Australia, prominent (and venerable) Kimberley pastoralist Michael Patrick Durack took up the cause. With the support of the Western Australian Government, the holdings of Connor Doherty and Durack Ltd (Argyle Downs, Auvergne, Ivanhoe and Newry stations) were valued and offered to the Freeland League for a large-scale farming and irrigation scheme. In December 1938, the Federal Government announced that Australia would admit 15,000 Jewish refugees from Austria and Germany over a three-year period. In fact, about 8000 arrived before the war.

While on a support-raising tour of Australia in May 1939, Freeland League secretary Dr I.N. Steinberg visited the Kimberley to assess the Durack scheme in the east Kimberley and an alternative proposal involving the Emanuel family's Fitzroy River holdings in the west Kimberley. Steinberg was more favourably impressed with the east Kimberley package,

which he envisaged would allow the settlement of some 75,000 Jewish refugees. However, the scheme never went ahead.

Three factors contributed to its demise. First, despite lobbying, it fell foul of the Federal Government's aversion to enclaves of non-British immigrants on Australian soil. Nor was it able to win strong support from Australian Jews. But perhaps the most decisive factor was that Dr Steinberg had had connections with Lenin and the Socialist-Revolutionary Party in Russia. In fact, he had been the first Commissar for Justice under Lenin. In 1944 (four years before the establishment of the modern state of Israel) the League was told that the plan would not be approved. By this time, the Western Australian Government's plans for the Ord River project, an alternative irrigation scheme also in the east Kimberley, were already well advanced.

CC

Dr I.N. Steinberg

Dwarfed by the MV Koolinda, two servicemen stand on the tidal flats under the Broome jetty on 4 May 1943. Throughout the Pacific war, the vulnerability of ships to enemy attack at low tide was a constant source of worry in Kimberley ports.

Primary Industry

"He's a Kimberley son" is perhaps the highest compliment a man can receive in this corner of Australia. There is an automatic implication that here is someone who was born in the area and has grown up with an intimate knowledge of this harsh and unforgiving country. But more than that, in this land of makeshift buildings and drifting lifestyles, it singles out someone whose family has made a commitment to the Kimberley. A "Kimberley son" (there is no equivalent expression for daughters) can be expected to have an understanding of a part of Australia that is as unique as the individuals who live there. Like their pioneering forebears, those now living in the Kimberley are still very close to the land and their life is still governed by the seasons.

Cattle Industry

An important part of the cultural fabric of Australia is the part played in its development by the Kimberley cattle kings (so well depicted by Dame Mary Durack in *Kings in Grass Castles* and *Sons in the Saddle*). The achievements of these almost legendary characters were described broadly in the chapter "Early European Settlement". Most of the Kimberley is still closely connected with the cattle industry.

The pastoral industry utilises 220,000 sq. km (about 64 per cent) of the Kimberley's 345,350 sq. km. However, despite the impressively large figures, less than 10 per cent of this grazing land can be regarded as high quality, particularly in the late dry season when there is a lack of feed. Variations in market price are also crucial here because of the high fixed costs of freighting to distant markets and the vagaries of climate. "Either the beef prices are good, or my cattle are," is the universal complaint of the land owner.

Many Kimberley pastoralists have found the uncertain nature of the industry unbearable and have sold up and moved out. The end result is that, over

Goaded along the race between road train and ship, a Shorthorn is on its way from Wyndham's dock to Sabah, Malaysia. Exporting to Asia is not new to the Kimberley: cattle were being shipped from Derby to Singapore back in 1887.

The all-purpose stockman's hat: An Aboriginal stockman from Pentecost Downs station uses his hat to take a drink from the Durack River. With their understanding of the land and ability to deal with the often harsh conditions, Aboriginal stockmen and station hands have played a vital role in developing the Kimberley.

the past quarter-century or so, the trend has been for ever-larger properties to be concentrated into fewer hands. This is partly due to economies of scale: it has been estimated that a Kimberley cattle station needs a minimum herd of 12,000 head to survive. Even so, most of the properties changing hands greatly exceed these marginal requirements. In 1963 there were 342 pastoral leases in the Kimberley; by 1983 the same amount of land was held under 93 leases (owned by only 63 companies), giving an average station area of about 350,000 ha.

During the lean years between 1978 and 1983 (when beef prices were low) more than half the Kimberley pastoral leases changed hands and the total herd size shrank by a quarter, with cattle numbers falling by 200,000 to about 650,000. Nevertheless, the Kimberley continues to carry about 40 per cent of all the cattle in WA.

Traditionally, Kimberley cattle stations have few fences: the cost of building them was regarded as prohibitive and unnecessary. (It's an oft-repeated Kimberley joke that the only time you can be sure you are eating your own beef is when you're at a barbecue at your neighbour's place.) A lot of cattle scattered over vast distances have in the past necessitated musters that were major logistical exercises and which resulted in many cattle being left to their own devices. The result is that the Kimberley cattle industry is

Rising above the encroaching vegetation, a tinplate cross marks the grave of pioneer stockman David Suttie. Unlike that of most of his peers, Suttie's memory lives on – he was Dan, the head stockman in Mrs Aeneas Gunn's 1908 classic We of the Never-Never, *in which she documents one year of her life on Elsey station near Katherine in the NT. In 1941, others who featured in the book were brought back and reburied at Elsey station. David Suttie remains where he died in 1912 – at his camp alongside the old Wyndham Road near "Black Rock Falls".*

much less developed than equivalent operations in the NT or Queensland.

However, this is changing, largely because of the greater control required under the tuberculosis eradication program. In a hard-hitting address in the Kimberley in 1986, Mr Brockman of the Pastoralists and Graziers Association of WA declared: "Open range management is a thing of the past unless you are content to become and remain a peasant farmer."

The reduction in the herd size has had its impact on the towns of the Kimberley too. Wyndham's large meatworks was opened in 1919 and was the largest single employer in tropical Australia after the Queensland sugar industry. The works employed 300 people and killed some 30,000 cattle each year. A decline in the number of cattle available for slaughter and industrial disputes led to the meatworks closing at the end of 1985. This was a heavy blow to the town and a large proportion of the population had to move elsewhere. Derby's small abattoirs had closed in 1979. Today, the Kimberley's only meatworks is at Broome, although abattoirs are being developed in Kununurra.

In 1985, the last year that the Wyndham meatworks operated, 45,000 Kimberley and 21,000 NT cattle were slaughtered at the Broome and Wyndham works. A further 44,000 were sent south for slaughter or sale, 23,000 were moved interstate (mainly for store or sale) and 5500 were shipped to Malaysia.

Today, there is also a shift towards live exports: there are regular shipments of cattle from Wyndham to Brunei and Sabah on the island of Borneo. About 100,000 cattle are sent out of the area to markets or meatworks in Australia or overseas each year. Kimberley beef is predominantly "hamburger beef" sold on the US market.

As herd control improves, some Kimberley stations are introducing Brahman or Afrikander cattle to replace the traditional Shorthorn. Advocates of the new breeds argue that they are more tick-resistant and the registered name of one, Droughtmaster, highlights another potential advantage, particularly after the poor wet seasons of the late 1980s.

The Kimberley cattle industry is just over 100 years old. It is going through a period of unprecedented reassessment and reorganisation. But few doubt that the industry that was the backbone of the Kimberley over its first century of European settlement will survive the next 100 years through a balance of conservation and exploitation of the land resources on which it is dependent.

The Ord River Project

It began as a dream and developed into a nightmare. However, incredible perseverance has seen the Ord River Project finally become a profitable venture.

The principle behind the Ord River Project is simple: 75,000 ha of rich clay soil needed only a year-round supply of water to become far more productive than it was as mere cattle pasture. The Ord River carries a huge volume of water from the Durack Range to the Cambridge Gulf, but nearly all the flow occurs during the wet season. The obvious solution was a dam that would ensure a regular water supply to the river flats downstream.

Kimberley Durack of Argyle Downs station provided the impetus for the scheme. He started cropping experiments on the Behn River in 1937 and his work was followed by the establishment of a State Government experimental farm on the Ord in 1942. Following successful production of cotton, sorghum and maize crops, the Kimberley Research Station was established as a joint federal/state project on the Ivanhoe Plain in 1945.

Results from the research station over the following years showed that sugarcane, rice, cotton, safflower and linseed grew well under irrigation. So, in 1958, more than 20 years after Kimberley Durack had made his attempts, the Ord River Project was born. The first stage (the diversion dam, irrigation system and the township of Kununurra) was completed in 1963 at a cost of $20 million. The Kununurra Diversion Dam raised the river level, enabling the Ivanhoe Plain to be irrigated without requiring water to be pumped. Three years later, there were 31 farms under irrigation.

The Ord River Dam, which created Lake Argyle, was completed in June 1972 at a cost of $22 million. One of the oldest homesteads in the area, Argyle Downs, established by the Durack family, would have been submerged when the lake filled, so it was moved to its present position and became a museum. Restrained by a dam wall 99 m high and 335 m long, Lake Argyle has a normal capacity of over 5.5 million cubic metres (nine times the volume of Sydney Harbour) and a surface area of 740 sq. km. In floods, the dam can hold nearly 35,000 million cubic metres and extends over an area of more than 2000 sq. km.

To prevent the lake filling with some 50,000 tonnes of silt flowing into it each wet season, in 1967 the Western Australian Government resumed and replanted the leases of several overgrazed cattle properties in the catchment area. This included the area around the Bungle Bungle Range.

Although over 50 kinds of crop have been tried under Ord irrigation since 1945, much of the early commercial cropping concentrated on cotton. However, attack by a chemical-resistant caterpillar and the removal of government subsidies killed off this industry in 1974. In the same year the Commonwealth Scientific and Industrial Research Organisation (CSIRO) took control of the Kimberley Research Station and the WA Department of Agriculture established its own research station nearby.

By the time cotton failed, rice seemed a good alternative. Although grown experimentally in the Kimberley since 1947, rice hadn't been commercially viable at first because a new variety was required to cope with the Kimberley climate and a zinc deficiency in the soil had to be overcome. This was achieved in the 1970s. However, as had happened with cotton, nature and economics conspired against the new crop. Birds, particularly magpie geese, flocked in for the feast the rice crops offered during the otherwise lean dry

There is still great scope for further development of the Ord River Project.

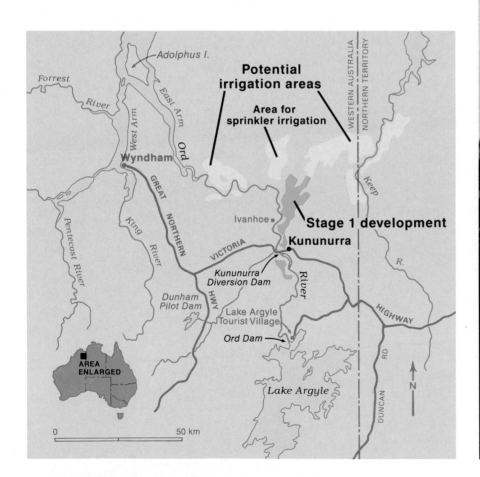

season. This depredation, combined with a weak market for rice, resulted in 1983 being the last year of commercial rice growing.

In 1987, the CSIRO's direct involvement in the Ord ended. The research station, the Frank Wise Institute of Tropical Agricultural Research, is now under Western Australian Government control. (Former State Premier Frank Wise was an enthusiastic champion of northern development.)

"The turning point for the Ord River Project came when the Government stopped handing out

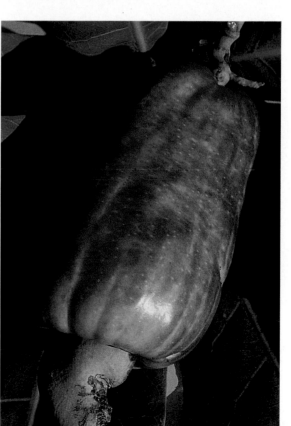

(Far left) Using her hand to indicate the grafting point of a cashew plant, horticulturist Christine Fitzgerald explains the process in a greenhouse on Ivanhoe Plain, near Kununurra. "To keep the quality of every planted cashew tree high, we graft the wood of a highly productive tree onto each seedling when it's about eight weeks old," she says. "The new plant then develops with the characteristics of the source tree."

(Left) The nut of the cashew tree is only a small appendage of the cashew fruit.

subsidies and each crop had to pay its own way," the regional manager of the Department of Agriculture, Dr Doug McGhie, argues. "We're a very long way from our markets: Perth is 3200 km and Brisbane more than 3500 km away, so we need good marketing and crops with high returns, such as cashews, peanuts and chickpeas. Kim-berley crops can fill a niche in out-of-season markets, too: bananas and rockmelons already do that. Overall, it's clear that a wide range of crops is better than a few major crops because that doesn't give pests the same foothold. The present largest money-earners reveal that diversity: bananas, grain sorghum, sunflower and

Farm worker Albert Snook takes some young grafted cashew plants out for planting. The cashew nut in its shell is only a small part of the harvest: some of the liquid from the nutshells produced in this isolated rustic setting will be compounded with other materials to form the heat-shielding nose-cones of spacecraft. More prosaically, the liquid is also used in vehicle brake linings, where it is released under heat and pressure, acting as a lubricant.

Converging towards infinity, rows of young soybeans fill a field in the Ord project area. Since 1978, soybeans have been a wet season crop. These are some of the first grown successfully during the dry season. Soybean oil is primarily used in food. It also has many other uses in products as diverse as paint, disinfectant, ink and soap.

rockmelons." A recent development has taken the Ord riverlands full circle. Irrigated pastures are providing feed for cattle-fattening prior to shipment. This is proving to be very profitable: once again, the banks of the Ord River are producing fodder for cattle. There is also a local dairy now.

Even so, with only 12,000 ha of a potential 75,000 ha being cultivated under the Ord River Project in 1988, a lot of development has yet to come. However, with profits of over $10 million in 1987, the development is finally paying its way, nearly 30 years after Kununurra was born to service it.

Mining

*(Right) Like an ants'
nest on the featureless
plains south-east of
Fitzroy Crossing,
Cadjebut mine tunnels
into underlying rock
strata. A relatively new
venture by BHP in
partnership with Shell,
Cadjebut zinc-lead
mine exported its first
shipment of zinc con-
centrate from Wyndham
in June 1988.*

*(Far right) Extracting
high-grade ore takes
precedence over the
million-dollar views at
BHP's Yampi mine on
Koolan Island. Like the
now-defunct iron ore
mine on nearby
Cockatoo Island, Yampi
mine has a limited life
span: at the current
extraction rate of
4 million tonnes a year
the ore body is expected
to be exhausted by
1993. Then the 800
people of the mining
community, the only
population centre of
any Kimberley island,
will disband.*

One corner of Derby airport is set aside as a check-in area for BHP employees going to the iron ore mine on Koolan Island. On the other side of the Kimberley, 70 workers fly from Kununurra to the Argyle Diamond Mine every day. It's an indication of the size and general inaccessibility of the Kimberley that mining companies here use aircraft the way mines in other areas use buses.

Koolan Island is in one of the most beautiful yet daunting places on Earth. It's in Yampi Sound, 130 km north of Derby. There, the Kimberley coast is a mass of islands and bays, long isthmuses and narrow channels where the land falls away to the outcrops of the Buccaneer Archipelago before finally surrendering to the Indian Ocean. This is a place of rugged beauty, high rainfall and tidal rips – and one of the richest iron ore bodies in the world.

The first Yampi ore was mined at nearby Cockatoo Island in 1951. When that mine closed in 1986, 31 million tonnes of ore had been extracted. Koolan Island, which employs 530 staff and produces 3.8 million tonnes per year, loaded its first shipment in 1965. Since then it has provided 50 million tonnes of high-grade ore for Japanese and Australian steelmakers. The ore reserves at Koolan Island are enough for mining to continue until the early 1990s. Shipping is certainly no problem: the open-cut mine is poised almost right on the edge of the wharf from which ore-carrying vessels are loaded. East of Fitzroy Crossing, Cadjebut mine (a joint BHP/Shell venture) is extracting lead-zinc ore. This underground mine is tapping into an ore body of some 2.5 million tonnes. The partly processed ore is trucked to Wyndham for export. Even with an annual output of about 350,000 tonnes, the mine will produce for another eight years. The majority

of the 120 employees of the mine work on a rotating basis, commuting from Broome by air for one week on/one week off.

Over 200 exploratory oil wells have pierced the Canning Basin so far but only four small fields, about 100 km south-east of Derby, are producing. The oil from these (Blina, Sundown, Lloyd and West Terrace) is piped from Blina to the highway and then trucked to Broome for shipping to the Kwinana refinery south of Fremantle. Output from these wells is relatively small – a total of about 100 kilolitres a day.

The Kimberley seems to hold the promise of future mineral riches: natural gas in the Bonaparte Basin and the Timor Sea; presently uneconomic deposits of 10 million tonnes of lead-zinc ore at Sorby Hills, 35 km north-east of Kununurra; and deposits of nickel at Sally Malay Bore, 185 km south-west of Kununurra, that are not currently economically viable. Alluvial gold is still being found around Halls Creek but not in large quantities. However, the Brockman's rare earth deposit near Halls Creek has great potential.

In the environmentally sensitive region of the Mitchell Plateau and Cape Bougainville to the east, huge reserves of bauxite have been discovered. The Mitchell Plateau has more than 235 million tonnes of ore with a commercially attractive concentration of 47.5 per cent alumina. Cape Bougainville has 980 million tonnes of 36 per cent alumina. At present, the depressed state of the world aluminium market has prevented development by a consortium of Comalco, Alcoa, Shell and others that still maintains the local road and airstrip. **DMcG**.

(Left) *The Argyle Diamond Mine cuts deeply into the southern end of the Ragged Range. Twenty million tonnes of rock had to be shifted to expose the 45 ha lamproite diamond-bearing pipe. Ore from the open-cut mine is dumped into the crushing plant on the hill then carried by conveyor belt to the main plant (beside the circular tanks used for water recovery) where it is crushed and separated. A concentrated, diamond-laden mixture goes into the high-security red-roofed building where the diamonds fluoresce under X-rays, activating air valves that blast them to one side.*

(Right) *Yielding a gram of diamonds for every tonne of rock, the primary stockpile has been through initial crushing but will be further reduced to pieces no larger than 6 mm. Security increases greatly along the processing line as the concentration of diamonds rises.*

(Inset) *Flanked by telephones, panel operators in the control room oversee the entire Argyle plant. Argyle is highly automated and controlled by computer – its software was developed in Australia. The whole operation is monitored by cameras, sensors and, ultimately, control room staff.*

With the discovery of diamonds near Lake Argyle, the Australian Kimberley found it had much more in common with its South African namesake than just boab (or baobab) trees. It is a strange coincidence that the Earl of Kimberley's name was given to two places that have some of the richest diamond fields in the world.

Australia's first diamonds were found in northern NSW and central Victoria in the latter half of last century. Some have also been discovered in South Australia, north-west Tasmania and southern Queensland but none of the deposits has been commercially viable. A few stones had been found in WA prior to 1979 but, again, nothing worth mining.

On 28 August 1979 the Perth laboratory of a prospecting venture found two diamonds in a sample from Smoke Creek in the Kimberley. The next day's sample had four stones in it, the following day's take had five. Following these traces, geologists walked onto and recognised the main diamond-bearing pipe on 2 October 1979. It is in a valley at the southern end of the Ragged Range, 35 km upstream from Lake Argyle.

The resulting Argyle Diamond Mine is owned by CRA Limited (56.8 per cent), Ashton Mining Group (38.2 per cent) and West Australian Trustees Limited (5 per cent). The mine, one of the most modern in the world, cost $465 million to build. Using X-ray recovery techniques and fully computerised operation, the mine will recover 30 million carats (about 6 tonnes) of diamonds per year for at least the next 20 years. That makes it the most productive diamond mine in the world. However, only 5 per cent of the diamonds mined are of gem quality. A further 40 per cent are in a category known as "cheap gem quality" and the remaining 55 per cent are industrial diamonds.

The diamonds are sent to Perth for sorting and sale. Some of the best gem-quality stones are now cut in Perth. Seventy-five per cent of the diamonds are sold through the Central Selling Organisation operated by De Beers, the international organisation that dominates the world diamond industry, and 25 per cent through Argyle's own office in Antwerp, Belgium.

Argyle diamonds are unique. They are harder than those found elsewhere and many are bronze or yellow in colour. The mine is also the world's only source of the rare and particularly valuable deep pink diamonds. One pink diamond has been valued at $1 million per carat while the top price for Argyle's white diamonds has been $18,000 per carat.

The only public access to the mine and the village is through a five-hour flying tour from Kununurra operated by Belray Diamond Tours. As one would expect, security is very tight in and around the mine area; there are also random body-searches on everyone leaving.

The mine works continually with two 12-hour shifts a day. However, conditions at the mine are far from unpleasant. "Club Argyle" is the nickname the 600 workers have given their living quarters in this remote part of the Kimberley more than 100 km from any town. Most of the mine staff commute from Perth by jet aircraft, staying at the mine for 14 days before heading back for 14 days off. The company mining village features dining rooms, bars, a sail-shaded swimming pool, several tennis courts and motel-style rooms for each worker.

Already there is some discussion about turning the Argyle Diamond Mine's accommodation into a holiday resort when the diamond-bearing pipe is exhausted. **DMcG**

The traditional image of pearling is of a rough-and-ready trade, pursued by gamblers, a trade in which every oyster holds the promise of a fortune, and death by misadventure awaits the careless. By comparison with this romantic image, pearling today is a very scientific profession, in which the oysters of the pearl farms are treated as carefully as pedigreed stock on a cattle station. But no matter how much the industry has changed since the days of the early pearlers, Broome is still one of the world's most important pearl centres. It has been since the 1890s.

Modern techniques of growing cultured pearls were developed in Japan, where early this century Kokichi Mikimoto was the leading pioneer. These techniques were introduced by the CSIRO to the Torres Strait pearl trade in 1949. The move was a good one: Australian oysters produce larger cultured pearls more quickly than Japanese oysters.

Cultured pearls are grown by opening the living oyster (in Australia, the gold-lip oyster, *Pinctada maxima*) and inserting a piece of mantle and an artificial "nucleus" into a cut made in the flesh of the oyster. The mantle is the lip of the oyster and it is this which produces the nacre, or pearl coating. The nucleus becomes the core of the cultured pearl. The right nucleus material is essential: the most common is the shell of the unfortunately named pig-toe clam from the Mississippi region of the United States.

Part of Cygnet Bay's annual harvest.

Pearling

A natural pearl is the result of the oyster dealing with an irritant, such as a grain of sand – or the nucleus. Although the oyster tries to eliminate the irritant, modern techniques ensure that over 80 per cent of the implants are successful and the nucleus stays in place. Failing to get rid of the irritant, the oyster uses the layer-building potential of the mantle to cover it. After three months, the oyster is taken out of the water and X-rayed to check that the nucleus has been retained.

A healthy Australian oyster will coat the nucleus in several layers of nacre each day. The pearl is ready about 18 months after implantation. It is then removed from the oyster and another nucleus inserted.

Most pearl farm oysters can produce two or three good pearls in a lifetime. After that, it's too old and the pearl too slow growing so its final cycle is dedicated to producing half-pearls. For this process several hemispherical nuclei are glued to the inside of the shell. At harvest time, the oyster must be killed because the half-pearls can only be removed by sawing them off the shell.

The largest cultured pearl farms in the Kimberley are at Kuri Bay, north of Derby. The bay was named in honour of Tokuichi Kuribayashi, whose Japanese company handles distribution and marketing of the pearls produced there by Pearls Pty Ltd. (Mr Kuribayashi became the most influential person in the Japanese pearl industry when Mr Mikimoto died.)

The first Kuri Bay pearls were produced in 1958 and the best single pearl so far has been an 18 mm flawless perfect round. The pearl was insured for $150,000 in 1980. It's not for sale.

Unlike the Kuri Bay operation, which is closely linked with Japan, the other long-established Kimberley pearl farm is an all-Australian venture. Bruce and Alison Brown have taken over the work of Bruce's father, Dean, who was a pioneer in cultured pearl farming in Australia along with Bruce's brother, Lyndon. The farm, at Cygnet Bay in King Sound, produced its first pearl in 1961. When Dean Brown died in 1980, his ashes were scattered on the headland overlooking the pearl leases he established. The farm is still flourishing, although, like others in Australia, it has had a high mortality rate among its oysters in recent years due to a disease which has swept through the industry, until recently resisting all efforts to control or prevent it. It's now preventable with careful husbandry.

Contrary to popular belief, the Broome pearl trade of the past had very little to do with pearls. A pearl was a very profitable bonus only for the lucky few. The real trade was in pearl shell, or mother-of-pearl (more commonly referred to by its initials, MOP). It was used mainly for buttons, cutlery handles and ornaments. In 1955, Australia was supplying 80 per cent of the world's requirements of MOP.

Commercial pearling commenced in Australia in the late 1860s at Shark Bay and Nickol Bay, WA. However, by the 1890s, operations had shifted north and Broome was the centre of the Western Australian pearling industry. Most of the divers in those first days were Aboriginal. But they were soon joined by "Malays" – a term then used generically to

The AUSTRALIAN GEOGRAPHIC team found this traditional heavy diving helmet in a Broome storeroom. Since Broome's last helmeted diver retired in 1975, helmets have become part of history. They were widely superseded by less clumsy hookah gear in the early 1970s.

Created by Spanish designer Carrera, this pearl pendant set with gold and diamonds highlights the beauty of its precious components.

describe anyone from Indonesia or Malaya – particularly after the Pearl Shell Fisheries Act of 1871 introduced some minimal safety standards to the industry. The new law prohibited the employment of women as divers: in those harsh times some had even been forced to dive in the final months of pregnancy.

These were the early days of "skindiving", when the divers regularly descended to depths of perhaps 18 metres or more without breathing apparatus. Even when regulations absolutely limited skindiving to 13 metres it was a rough trade and many divers didn't survive a season.

But technological progress produced a more insidious danger than sharks and overwork. Helmeted diving gear was introduced to the Kimberley between 1884 and 1887. It took some years before the cause of decompression sickness (which occurred all too regularly) was understood and "staged ascents" introduced to avoid nitrogen bubbling out of the body tissues after a diver surfaced. This is similar to the way bubbles form when the cap is removed from a bottle of fizzy soft drink. The syndrome is popularly known as "the bends" because it commonly occurs in joints like elbows and knees.

The industry was booming. Japanese divers had replaced Aborigines and by 1903 Broome had a fleet of 300 pearling vessels, all taking shell from ever-greater depths. Between 1909 and 1917 Broome recorded 145 deaths from "diver's paralysis". Many other divers finished their days permanently crippled from the destructive effects of the nitrogen bubbles.

Broome received its first decompression chamber (the world's first) in 1913. The device is still on display in Bedford Park. By 1918 Broome divers were following Admiralty diving tables and the death rate had dropped dramatically.

Although pearl shell was the mainstay of the industry, a good-quality pearl could make a pearler rich. The diver who found it also received a share of the profit. Such rewards were rare – only one oyster in thousands has a pearl and less than 1 per cent of those pearls are gem quality. Even so, some struck it rich.

The best natural pearl taken from the Kimberley oyster beds is the "Star of the West", a drop-shaped pearl about the size of a sparrow's egg. It was found in 1917 and sold for £6000.

The "Southern Cross" is Australia's most famous pearl: it's a formation of nine pearls in the shape of a crucifix. It was found by a young boy cleaning shell near Broome in 1883. One of several stories about its origins tells how, when it was found, it was broken in three pieces and sold by the lugger skipper for £10. It was reassembled (with the addition of a ninth pearl to make the shape more balanced) and valued at £10,000 in 1924. It's now in the Vatican collection.

Plastic buttons came on the market after World War II and heralded the demise of the traditional mother-of-pearl button. By 1958, the MOP industry was in the doldrums. There had been ups and downs in the market before, but by 1960 Australian pearling was saved only by the advent of the cultured pearl industry.

Diving for oysters is still an integral part of the pearl industry. The oysters required for the pearl farms are collected from naturally occurring pearl beds by divers. Indeed, until 1974 most divers were still using the old-style diving suits with helmets. However, when it was established that a diver using lightweight hookah equipment could work more effectively, the Broome pearlers adopted the newer technology. Hookah resembles scuba gear except the diver doesn't wear tanks but relies on a hose link to tanks and compressor on the vessel above. The luggers gave way to progress, too. Most pearling is now done from modern steel boats (even some multi-hulled craft) rather than the traditional wooden vessels. Although more efficient, the steel ships, with their hookah divers, don't have the same mystique as an old lugger with helmeted divers.

Fortunately there are still a lot of copper helmets in shops, stores and museums around Broome and a few old pearling luggers to be seen. Although visitors can still buy pearl shell, the emphasis these days is on cultured pearls. In beautiful juxtaposition, Broome pearls are now found in settings alongside Argyle diamonds. Pearling techniques may have changed and Broome may no longer run on a schedule dictated by the movement of the pearling fleet, but the industry remains very much a part of life in the Kimberley today. **DMcG**

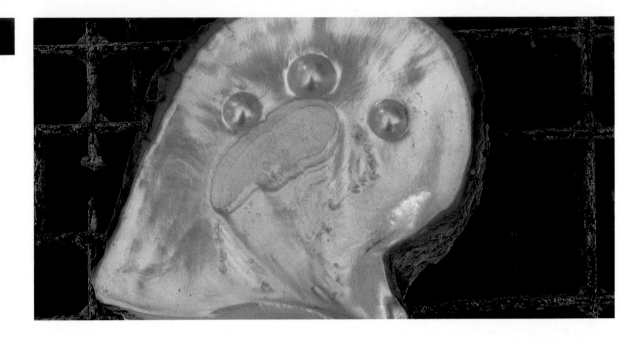

The hemispheres on this pearl shell are the oyster's death warrant. When a mollusc ages and its production of nacre slows, nuclei for inexpensive half-pearls are glued to the inside of the shell. When the nuclei are sufficiently coated, the oyster is killed and the half-pearls sawn off.

Intense concentration shows on the face of Kikotaka Hattori as he removes a pearl from an oyster prior to placing another nucleus within its flesh. This must be done accurately and without disturbing the oyster unduly. The Kimberley pearling industry today is a precise, highly scientific industry. Like the majority of technicians, Kikotaka is Japanese and was trained in the cultured pearl industry in Japan. He has lived on the Kimberley coast since 1979.

Royal Flying Doctor Service

A large locked cupboard occupies most of one wall of the bathroom at Fossil Downs station, near Fitzroy Crossing. It's a facility repeated in many homesteads throughout the Kimberley: each one contains the ubiquitous Royal Flying Doctor Service of Australia Medical Chest. In most cases, the medicines are supplied free of charge "to be kept handy to your receiver". Even at Fossil Downs, in one of the more populous parts of the Kimberley, the radio is close at hand in the office just along the veranda. The nearest Flying Doctor base is in Derby, 300 km away.

In the chest there is a wide range of medicines, each with the name and a number clearly displayed. In this land where medical help may be hours away, even by aircraft, self-treatment that goes a long way beyond first aid may be required. There is also a simple chart and notes to help the lay-person explain pain and symptoms for diagnosis over the radio.

The great advantage of these standardised medical chests is

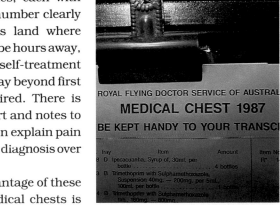

ROYAL FLYING DOCTOR SERVICE OF AUSTRAL
MEDICAL CHEST 1987
BE KEPT HANDY TO YOUR TRANSC

Tray	Item	Amount	Item No
B D	Ipecacuanha, Syrup of, 30ml, per bottle	4 bottles	R* 1
3 B	Trimethoprim with Sulphamethoxazole, Suspension 40mg. — 200mg. per 5mL, 100mL per bottle	1 bottle	
4 B	Trimethoprim with Sulphamethoxazole tab., 160mg. — 800mg.		

that they enable doctors to administer treatment by remote control. Even someone who is medically illiterate can dish out two tablets of number 62 (from tray B) or smear on some 139 (from tray A) as instructed by the doctor.

The real genius of the Royal Flying Doctor Service is the utilisation of technology to spread a "mantle of safety" over the vastness of remote Australia. That phrase was coined by the Reverend John Flynn, of the Australian Inland Mission, whose Flying Doctor Service started in May 1928, when a plane flew from Cloncurry, Queensland to a small bush hospital. However, the technological development that enabled the service to become viable came a few years later when the pedal radio was invented by Alfred Traeger, an Adelaide electrician. This made it possible for just one person to operate a self-contained morse transmitter with a range of almost 500 km. For the first time, people on remote stations could be in instant contact with a doctor.

Medical treatment by numbers: simple, clever ideas are a hallmark of the RFDS. Just as using aircraft was the logical solution to the vast distances of outback Australia, a comprehensive medical cabinet (right) and the easily interpreted list of contents supported by a symptoms questionnaire near the radio transceiver enables the untrained to administer suitable medication under instruction.

(Far right) A faded sign in Derby traces the illustrious history of the RFDS. Initiated by the Australian Inland Mission in 1927, the service was handed over to citizens' groups in 1934. The first RFDS association was established in Victoria to administer the Kimberley region. Today, head office remains in Melbourne, close to its funding base rather than its area of operations on the far side of the continent.

In the 1930s the Australian Inland Mission handed the flying doctor operation over to a non-denominational honorary body, the Royal Flying Doctor Service, which has sections in several States. The Victorian section, the first one to be established (in 1934), doesn't have any "outback" in its own State so it accepted responsibility for the most remote part of Australia: the Kimberley.

In the Kimberley, there are Royal Flying Doctor bases at both Wyndham and Derby, but the main radio base is at Derby and the large hangar at Derby airport houses a range of aircraft to suit most remote airstrips. If the Derby or Wyndham hospitals can't deal with the illness or injury, the patient will normally be flown to a hospital in Perth.

Today, most of the medicinal aviation is preventive, not surgical, and takes the form of clinics conducted in remote Aboriginal communities. These are attended by a flight sister and one or two doctors who see about 600 patients a month. Even in emergencies, the aircraft are used as aerial ambulances not surgeries. Very rarely are surgical operations done on the site.

Until 1987 there were about 100 outback stations tuned into the RFDS radio network, which provided both a social link and an emergency service. However, the introduction of the microwave telephone changed this system. By the end of 1988, nearly all Kimberley stations had microwave telephones and the RFDS radio link is now mainly used in conjunction with mobile radios carried by travellers or by exploration parties.

Patients don't pay to use the RFDS – its operating costs are largely covered by the Western Australian and Federal Governments. The State Government pays the wages of medical personnel while up to half the cost of aircraft and some related equipment is met by the Federal Government. The balance is met by donations, bequests and fund-raising in both Victoria and the Kimberley.

The Flying Doctor has played a vital part in opening up the Kimberley by providing much-needed security to families whose nearest neighbours may be 100 km or more away.

In the wet season, many of the small airstrips become unusable after heavy rain. Peter Harradine, the regional manager for the Kimberley RFDS, told me that to check the state of the strip, station owners are asked to drive along it at between 60 and 80 km/h.

"If they can do that without skidding or sinking, our pilots will probably find it okay when they arrive. It saves wasted flights."

If all else fails, one of the Kimberley's few helicopters can be called upon in an emergency. To the city dweller, the RFDS is a clever response to the problems posed by the distances in remote Australia. In the outback, it's a much appreciated lifeline. **DMcG**.

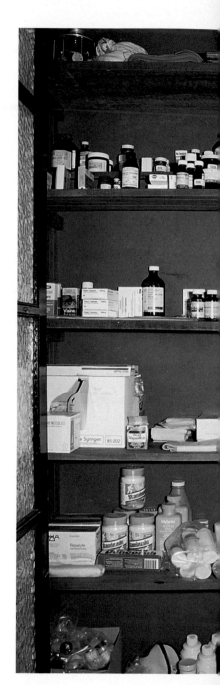

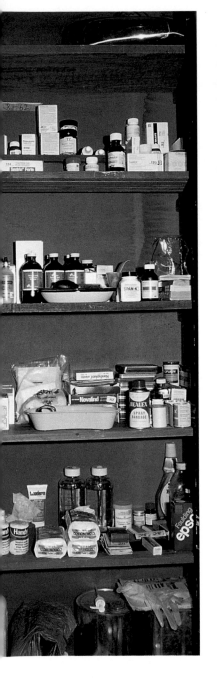

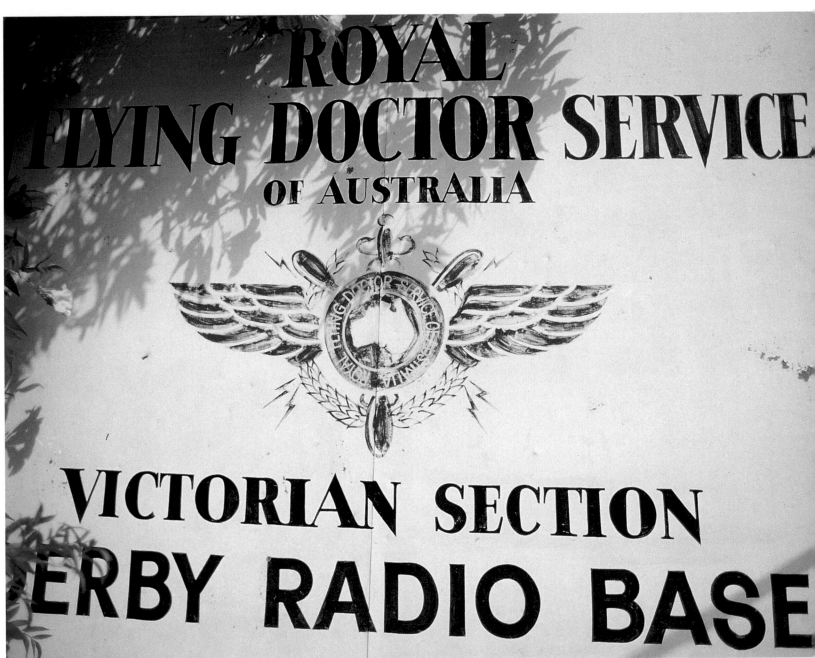

*Surrounded by all the normal trappings of a primary school, teacher Colleen O'Rourke **(left)** speaks to a classroom larger than Japan or Norway. The pupils' desks are, in effect, the pigeonholes **(above right)** where assignments are posted and received as often as infrequent mail services allow.*

It looks just like any small country school – brightly coloured children's paintings cover the walls, books and mobiles abound. However, apart from the infrequent visitor in town for a day or two, few of this school's 40 students see it more than once or twice a year.

This is the Kimberley School of the Air, based in Derby, and its "classroom" spreads out over the whole Kimberley. It gives lessons to children from pre-primary school age through to Year 7 on stations from Ord River in the east, Drysdale River in the north and Bohemia Downs in the south. On weekdays, each class has an on-air time of between 30 and 40 minutes. Classes themselves are limited to six students, "otherwise the children wouldn't receive enough individual attention," says relieving school principal Janette Grieve.

"Has everyone finished colouring in the countries that would fit inside Western Australia?" teacher Colleen O'Rourke asks her Year 4 class. "If so, let's move on to looking at the water cycle."

The day I sat in on classes at the school, education had a certain direct, if poignant, relevance. The water cycle of the Kimberley governs much of the pupils' lives: from the isolation of the wet season, with its dramatic thunderstorms and torrential rains, to the heartbreak of droughts, when the Wet doesn't provide enough rain to last through the next dry season. And the school itself owes its existence to the size of Western Australia – this "classroom" is larger than many countries.

The School of the Air is a triumph of ingenuity over daunting logistics. It works

through the Flying Doctor radio: "We were given our own frequency in 1982," Janette says. "From about 1960 [when the school started] until then, we were on the same frequency as the RFDS, so classes were disrupted every time there was an emergency." The school, next door to Derby High School, is part of the Western Australian Ministry of Education and, as in other schools, the education is free. Classroom material (everything from texts to calculators, sports kits and guitars) is generally sent out by mail every week and assignments are sent in just as frequently for marking.

However, some stations have a much less frequent mail service and some have none at all and must either arrange to have the mail sent out from town or must go in and collect it.

For a week each year, the students and their "home tutors" (the mothers in most cases) meet the teachers from Derby. Although it is a good chance for the children to see what the other kids behind the voices in the class look like, this is mainly a chance for the home tutors to be given assistance and guidance by the teachers. Once a year, all the senior students (who are within a few years of going to boarding school) spend two weeks in Perth with other students and teachers from the five divisions

of the School of the Air in WA. Direct personal contact is also given by an itinerant teacher who visits each student in turn. For the rest of the year, school is a microphone and the teacher is a loudspeaker. Even so, close relationships exist between the teachers and their distant charges.

"The greatest sin any School of the Air teacher can commit is to be in an area near a student and not visit," Janette Grieve says. "This year when I called in to see a couple of students their father claimed my arrival had been awaited with even more anticipation than Santa Claus." **DMcG**

Kimberley Towns

The street is crowded as patrons leave Sun Pictures, Broome's open-air picture theatre, after the Saturday night show. Sun Pictures first opened its doors in 1916 when an evening at the "flicks" was a novelty and the images did, indeed, flicker. It has been operating continually ever since and has changed little over the years. Audiences still sit in canvas deckchairs or on benches and rain can bring the session to a halt. Spring tides once posed a greater threat – until a levee bank was built, theatregoers often found the floor awash when session times and high tide coincided.

It's fitting that the last part of Highway One to be sealed was the 275 km stretch between Halls Creek and Fitzroy Crossing. Work on this section of the 16,000 km road that largely follows the periphery of the continent was started in 1974 and officially opened 12 years later, in September 1986. For the Kimberley region it was much more than the final link in a chain around Australia; the all-weather road was an important step in Kimberley development. Greatly increased numbers of tourists have come flooding along the bitumen and transporting cattle and ore out of the region has become much easier and more reliable.

As the Kimberley settles into the second hundred years of European settlement, it looks set to realise its potential. However, development may result in a very different Kimberley from today's, with its endearing close links with the past. Nowhere are the first signs of this change so clearly evident as in

the towns of the region and the ebb and flow between them. While Broome and Kununurra are moving ahead, Derby and Wyndham aren't developing much at all. Meanwhile, Halls Creek remains an enigmatic mixture of the past and the future.

Broome

Walking the bustling streets of Broome or standing at a bar listening to tales of tourist development and soaring housing prices, it's hard to imagine that the town was long held to have no potential at all. Indeed, after Broome was gazetted on 27 November 1883, the man after whom it was named, the Governor of WA, Sir Frederick Napier Broome, wrote to the Colonial Secretary to complain: "I believe the town named after me ... is likely to remain a mere 'dummy' townsite inhabited by the tenants of three graves ... My present idea is to have the name cancelled." He

Gilded by the morning sun, oil storage tanks that supply the fuel needs of the west Kimberley are reflected in a roadside pool at Entrance Point outside Broome. Oil tankers from the BP refinery at Kwinana, near Perth, fill these tanks before continuing to Wyndham and Darwin.

A pagoda-topped telephone booth and a street sign in English, Japanese, Chinese, Malay and Arabic stand on the corner of Carnarvon and Short streets, Broome, testament to the multiculturalism that has been a feature of the town since it was established in the 1880s.

didn't get his way and, in an ironic twist of fate, few have any idea after whom the famous town was named.

For much of Broome's more than 100 years of existence, the town has been known as "the Port of Pearls". When plastic buttons largely replaced pearl shell after World War II and the pearling industry went into decline, so too did Broome. Even so, in 1954 Broome (with a population then of about 1100) was still being described as a "rip-roaring shanty town". Today Broome has a population of around 7000 people and hasn't

lost any of its rowdiness – although now the crowds around town are more likely to be tourists than pearl divers.

Broome has one important feature that is lacking in all other Kimberley towns. It possesses sandy beaches. Cable Beach and the other strips of pristine sand stretching north towards Beagle Bay may be the basis of Broome's future growth. The development of the luxury Cable Beach Club and Roebuck Bay Resort has certainly marked a turning point for what was once a shanty town!

Buccaneer Rock, a patch of green vegetation and red rock standing out of the mudflats of Roebuck Bay, retains traces of its early use as an important navigation aid for luggers coming into the Streeters & Male jetty at Broome. With the decline of lugger traffic and the construction of the deep water port at Entrance Point in 1966, the beacon fell into disuse; today neither light nor bell remain. The region's strong links with William Dampier are clear in nomenclature: the bay is named after Dampier's ship, the rock after his reputation as a buccaneer.

A stark reminder of the early days of pearling, when divers were pressed to the limit of their physical endurance, a Japanese gravestone in the Broome cemetery highlights the harsh consequences of misjudgement.

Cable Beach takes its name from the international telegraph cable that came ashore here from Java which, in turn, was linked to London. The line, opened in 1891, supplemented the original London–Australia link through Palmerston (now Darwin). A transmitting station was built in Broome; it is now the courthouse. With its large verandas and sloping roof, the building remains a superb example of northern Australian architecture.

Broome's multilingual street signs (which include English, Malay, Chinese, Japanese and Arabic script) and Orient-inspired telephone booths point to the town's cosmopolitan past. The Aboriginal, Indonesian, Filipino, Malay, Japanese and Chinese workers in the pearling industry have certainly left an indelible cosmopolitan stamp on the town.

After Broome was bombed in World War II, there was strong local anti-Japanese feeling but in 1952 the Australian Government issued a specific exemption to the "White Australia Policy" so that Japanese divers could return to Broome to revive the pearling industry. Balancing the memory of those who died in the air raids, Broome's Japanese cemetery is a poignant reminder of the Japanese contribution to Broome and pearling. The Shinju Matsuri (Festival of the Pearl) in Broome each August is an annual acknowledgement of the bond between Broome and the pearlers of Japan.

Broome today is a very unusual country town. There are very few small towns in Australia (or anywhere else, for that matter) that have several shops stocking single pieces of jewellery worth tens (and even hundreds) of thousands of dollars. In Broome it seems that every second shop sells pearls. The casually dressed holiday crowds must have more money than their shorts and T-shirts suggest: the exquisite Broome pearls on display sell well despite their high values and astronomical price tags.

There is a cultural richness to Broome that appeals to every visitor. New colonial-style buildings and the sleepy Chinatown, the rambling Streeters & Male store from Broome's first days, Sun Pictures (an operating open-air picture theatre dating back to 1916) and pearling luggers tied up at the old jetty all contribute to the feeling.

The unique attractions of the town and its surrounding areas are many. In the sandstone of the water's edge at Gantheaume Point are the petrified footprints of a carnivorous dinosaur that lived 100 million years ago. These are revealed during low spring tides. Less extreme tides reveal the corroding hulks of the flying boats that were sunk in the air raid of 1942. There's even the faint promise of hidden treasure: an extremely unlikely legend has it that William Dampier buried a sea chest here when careening his vessel and there is the more tangible mystery of the "Flight of Diamonds" (see page 80).

Broome is the Kimberley's southern gateway and the region's seaside resort. Huge sums are being spent developing tourism. About 50,000 travellers arrive each year and not all of them leave. Throughout its history many casual visitors to Broome have decided to stay. As a result, this town continues to grow faster than anywhere else in the Kimberley.

Broome courthouse (left) and Cable Beach (far left) are remnants of the era of the first telegraphic communications. Australia's first direct link with London (through Palmerston, now Darwin) was supplemented by another cable from Java. It came ashore at Cable Beach, then joined the new overland telegraph line to Perth. Today, Cable Beach is the site of a thriving tourist area with resort, zoo and crocodile park. In 1889, what is now the courthouse building was prefabricated in Singapore, shipped to the Kimberley in sections and erected as the Roebuck Bay Cable Station, serving in that role until March 1914. It remained disused for several years before coming into use as the local courthouse.

Derby

From the air, my first view of Derby was of a long finger of land stretching out into the paisley pattern of the King Sound mudflats. The town is scattered along the peninsula and the famous Derby wharf reaches out to seek deep water off the point.

On landing, we were greeted by the sight of fat boabs dusted with a snow-like covering of thousands of corellas, the ubiquitous white cockatoos of the north.

Leaving the aircraft near the Flying Doctor hangar, we walked out to the road seeking a way into town. "G'day. You must be David McGonigal. I'm Norm Longden and this is your rental car."

The man standing by a 4WD walked over with a smile. I was incredulous. "How on earth did you know when we'd arrive?" I asked.

"I found out your aircraft call sign from the office in Perth and asked air traffic control to give me a call when you were coming in," he replied.

There's an outgoing helpfulness in the Kimberley generally that is astounding to the city dweller and it's a particularly appealing feature of Derby: this is the town that extended credit to the first pastoralists. Derby (pronounced "Durby" not "Darby" as in England) has long held the title of the market town for the west Kimberley. Broome (gazetted on the same day: 27 November 1883) may have had the flash pearlers but Derby was

Reflections in a shop window mirror the wharf end of the Derby township. The house on the other side of the road, built in the traditional style of northern Australia, is being renovated as part of a council heritage project. Like a lot of buildings in Derby, it has a boab tree as a neighbour. The 4WD out the front is representative of the many 4WDs that form a large proportion of Kimberley traffic. Although it is possible to travel many of the roads in the area by conventional vehicle, some out-of-the-way places can be reached only by 4WD.

the port of the west Kimberley and the service town for the pastoral and grazing industries. It was named after Lord Derby who, like the Earl of Kimberley, was a Secretary of State for the Colonies.

Unfortunately, Derby's port on King Sound has always proved difficult for shipping. There are savage tidal rips at the entrance and both the channel and wharfside are virtually dry at the lowest extreme of the 10 m tidal range. Unlike early vessels, modern ships are not designed to sit on their bottoms and that, combined with silting problems in the Derby channel, has caused port use to decline markedly since the early 1980s. The first Derby jetty was opened in 1885, two years after the Yeeda station wool clip was washed away by the tsunami (giant wave) caused by the eruption of Krakatau. In 1902, the horse-drawn tramway was extended along the 4 km causeway to the jetty, a great advantage in moving cargo. That original jetty stood for 79 years before finally being replaced in 1964. Today the new wharf is well on the way to becoming just an historic landmark and fishing platform – it was last used by a commercial vessel in 1983.

Derby developed quickly at the time of the Halls Creek gold rush but soon had to compete with the new port of Wyndham that opened up closer to the goldfields in 1886. The town has always been a communications centre: the first air-mail service in Australia was between Geraldton and Derby in 1921, largely overcoming the communication difficulties created by the inaccessibility of this northern region. Derby is still the major airfreight destination in the Kimberley.

The most important institution in Derby today is the hospital, which is the largest in the Kimberley and is integrated with the operations of the Derby base of the Royal Flying Doctor Service.

An important development has recently boosted Derby's profile. Yeeda station, 40 km to the south, the first enduring grazing property to be established in the west Kimberley, is now the site of a $64 million Curtin RAAF base which also acts as the commercial airport and has potential as an international passenger airport.

Today, Derby's population of 5000 is an open-hearted community living in an open-plan town of wide, boab-shaded streets. For travellers, it's the stepping off point for the "Gibb River Road" and the many natural features along the way, including Tunnel Creek and Windjana Gorge. Locals continue to see it as the long-standing administrative and service centre for the west Kimberley.

Fitzroy Crossing

In the middle of the dry season, the 1200 people who live in Fitzroy Crossing must sometimes feel besieged by tourists. Over 50,000 travel through town each year and 25,000 of them turn off the highway to visit Geikie Gorge, 12 km to the north. To anyone passing straight through, Fitzroy Crossing is a scattering of buildings on the northern side of the highway, with the roadhouse the most notable feature. The community lies at the foot of the central Kimberley hills. To the west, the Fitzroy flood plain spreads towards the mouth of the river where it runs into the vastness of King Sound.

Turning onto the Geikie Gorge road reveals the predominantly Aboriginal community of Fitzroy Crossing spreading over several kilometres along the banks of the Fitzroy River. The river continues to dictate life here. Named after Robert Fitz-Roy, a captain of the *Beagle* before its voyages along the Kimberley coast, the river's catchment area is 45,300 sq. km (compared to the Ord's 46,200 sq. km). When the river is in flood, about 100 million cubic metres of water may flow past Fitzroy Crossing each hour (enough to fill Sydney Harbour in five hours) and the Crossing Inn, situated right on its banks, is regularly inundated.

"We let the staff go then and spend a lot of time on table tops," says Peter Sandford, who manages the hotel. For most of the other half of the year the river is merely a series of waterholes. In this fluvial "feast-or-famine" environment, water for the town is supplied from a bore.

Fitzroy Crossing took a decade to come into being as the great Australian triumvirate: a police station, telegraph office and pub. The settlement remains vital today. The Sunday "session" at the Crossing Inn is legendary throughout the Kimberley – the open-air dance floor is packed with a polyglot crowd from the town and surrounding stations. Minus the rock music it could be the Kimberley any time in the past hundred years.

Halls Creek

One shouldn't expect modern Halls Creek to show any signs of the boom town that did so much to establish the Kimberley: the township moved from the site of original settlement to its present position in the early 1950s. This was to better allow for further expansion, to take advantage of a more reliable water supply and to give it room for an airstrip. From 2000 or more at the time of the gold rush, Old Halls Creek's population had fallen

to 300 by then. A string of shops along the highway and a grid of streets to the south is the unusual layout of the new town, which has grown a lot over the past 15 years. It still has the feel of an inland, outback town; you don't smell the tang of a sea breeze from the distant coast, just the ever-present desert dust.

I first stayed in Halls Creek in 1986 and, although comfortable, the rooms at the Kimberley Hotel-Motel next to the airstrip were basic Kimberley accommodation. Returning in 1988, I noticed that the hotel entrance had been redesigned and there was a well-appointed restaurant where before there had been only a simple dining room. My comments on this led the receptionist to reply: "Wait until you see

your rooms – you'll think you've died and gone to heaven." The well-finished room was so far removed from the old Kimberley approach of merely "making do" that I had to assess Halls Creek anew.

While the wooden beams and mud-brick walls of the original goldmining town crumble away, the new Halls Creek is experiencing its own boom as the sealed highway brings more visitors to the town. There is potential for another mining boom to revitalise the town, too. This time the minerals are rare earths rather than gold, and development will be in one large operation rather

As one looks south-west over the Great Northern Highway to Halls Creek and beyond, the flat terrain surrounding the Kimberley's most inland town is readily apparent. In 1948, the townspeople voted to move from the original makeshift town to the current site, which has the advantages of good water supply, room for expansion and is close to the aerodrome and highway. The shift also resulted in new civic buildings to replace the simple mud-brick buildings of the early gold town.

Somnolent in the late afternoon sun, boabs outnumber vehicles on MacPhee Street, which leads to Wyndham wharf. Since Lieutenant Phillip Parker King sailed the Mermaid *into Cambridge Gulf in September 1819, Wyndham has had a chequered history. It was established for, and boomed with, the Kimberley gold rush, becoming a cattle port after the gold rush. The mainstay of Wyndham for most of this century was the meatworks, opened in 1919. However, economic forces closed the meatworks in late 1985. Today, road trains rattle down the main street as they bring live cattle for shipping to Asian markets and southern Western Australia.*

than individuals digging for dreams.

In several ways, Halls Creek is unusual. It's the only Kimberley town on a road junction and it's the largest one to be located far from the coast (Kununurra isn't far from the mouth of the Ord River). This town, with a population of 1350 people, most of them Aboriginal, marks the point where Highway One is joined by the Duncan Road and, just west of town, by the Tanami Track coming from Alice Springs past Wolfe Creek Meteorite Crater. Its location and altitude (400 m above sea-level) give Halls Creek a more pleasant climate than that experienced by other towns in the Kimberley. It has less rain in the wet season and experiences generally cooler nights throughout the year.

Wyndham

"Imagine hang gliding off here. You could fly up and down this ridge all day and never get tired of the view," said photographer Robbi Newman as we stood on top of Five Rivers Lookout at the summit of The Bastion Range, about 300 m above Cambridge Gulf. Wyndham's port seemingly lay at our feet and we could trace the courses of the Ord, King, Pentecost, Forrest and Durack rivers

At first sight, the enclosing arc of Wyndham wharf resembles sea baths but its population of saltwater crocodiles would deter the most enthusiastic swimmer. Wyndham's first public wharf, built in 1890, was close to town at Anthon Landing. The current wharf site was first used in 1919 to serve the new meatworks and was extended in 1959. In 1971, because of rising costs and better road links, State Shipping Services cancelled the passenger services between Fremantle and Darwin which called at Wyndham. It remains an active cargo port.

Cracked into a mosaic by fierce sunlight, a road sign on the outskirts of Kununurra points the way towards the NT. Kununurra is the easternmost town of the Kimberley – from here, the road runs east, north of Lake Argyle, to cross the border near the Victoria River.

as they flowed into the gulf. It's a beautiful view and puts the town of Wyndham in perspective: a tiny community clinging to the strip of land between the hills and the edge of Cambridge Gulf. The scars of the recently removed meatworks are still clearly visible.

In 1986, Wyndham had its centenary. Sadly, instead of being a time of celebration, the centenary year marked a low point: the year after the meatworks closed. The closure of the meatworks, with a staff of 300 by far the largest employer in Wyndham, had forced many residents to leave town and seek work elsewhere. In 1988, two years later, as a poignant reminder of these events, Wyndham's giant wooden birthday cake still lay abandoned at Wyndham port within sight of the vacant block where the meatworks stood.

Wyndham is really two towns about 5 km apart and linked by a sealed road that skirts the edge of the Cambridge Gulf mudflats. Most of the 1200 people who live here have houses at what is still almost universally referred to by locals as the "Three Mile", while the main points of interest for tourists are clustered around the port. The reason for the two towns is topographical: as the population grew, there was no room to accommodate the newcomers at the port, which is squeezed between the gulf and a steep sandstone ridge, so they settled at a point on the track about three miles inland from the port. In 1968, the Three Mile Settlement officially became part of Wyndham.

The gold rush at Halls Creek provided the impetus for the establishment of Wyndham. When it was declared a townsite on 2 September 1886, the first lots of land at the port sold with a reserve of £50 each. It was named Wyndham by John Forrest (later Lord) after the son of Lady Barker, wife of Sir Frederick Napier Broome, Governor of WA. A shortage of fresh water at the port saw

settlements and camps spring up at the 20-mile post and at three-mile (about five-kilometre) intervals between the 12-mile post and the port as miners came for supplies and, later, pastoralists brought cattle down for shipment to Fremantle or South-East Asia. Apart from the "Three Mile", these communities no longer exist. After the gold rush, the town languished until 1919 when the meatworks opened. Until its closure in November 1985, the works provided

one of Australia's most unusual and grisly tourist attractions: large saltwater crocodiles waiting at the outflow of the works' blood drain.

Today, most croc-spotting takes place from the wharf, with good chances of success. Wyndham's limited appeal as a bathing spot is not enhanced by the baleful stare of a big "salty" sunbathing below the supports of the wharf. When one looks out from the wharf at low tide, there is a swirling in the water that some new arrivals take to be an indication of the presence of crocodiles in the water. It isn't: it's a part of Wyndham's history. In World War II Wyndham was bombed on only one occasion and suffered little damage. However, in a separate attack, the *Koolama*, a State Shipping Service vessel, was hit on its way out of Darwin and, disabled, made its way to Wyndham where it sank upside down near the wharf. It remains a significant hazard for every ship using the port.

Wyndham is surrounded by rivers and water and is unique in being the only town in the Kimberley not supplied from a bore. It relies on the King River pools in the dry season and Moochalabra Dam in the Wet. The water from both is pumped about 20 km over the tidal flats to storage tanks near town. Another waterhole fulfils a more picturesque function: Marlgu Billabong, a bird sanctuary 15 km from the port, is home to pelicans, brolgas, jabirus, cranes, herons and innumerable magpie geese. At dawn, the enthusiastic bird watcher can come close to many species that are only seen from afar elsewhere in the north.

The port of Wyndham still has much of the atmosphere of an old Kimberley town. Boabs line the main street and most of the action centres around the pub and Grandison's hardware store. It remains the port of the east Kimberley, just as Broome is for the west Kimberley: at Wyndham supplies come in, ore and cattle go out.

Travellers must detour off Highway One to visit Wyndham. Those who do will find a strong spirit of the pioneering Kimberley that has largely disappeared in the more sophisticated faster-growing towns.

Kununurra

Like Canberra before it, Kununurra was designed and built to a plan. It was created in the early 1960s to service the Ord River Irrigation Area but it has since developed as a regional centre in its own right, replacing Wyndham as the centre for the east Kimberley.

The traveller gets quite a surprise coming into Kununurra from the Victoria Highway. The town of just over 3600 people is well planned and neat. Other Kimberley towns just grew over the years and their town plans are largely the result of

Nestled between the Ord River and the rocky outcrops of Hidden Valley, Kununurra has a planned, modern look that is not found in other Kimberley towns. That's because Kununurra was deliberately created in the 1950s as the service town for the Ord River Project. By contrast, every other Kimberley community just drifted into being and grew haphazardly. The cluster of large buildings in the middle of the photograph is the shopping centre. The town's name comes from "cununurra", the Aboriginal name for the Ord River, literally meaning "big water".

historical accident. However, Kununurra existed on a drawing board long before the first house or road was built. While new development has seen the township spill across to the south of the Victoria Highway, the town is still largely centred around a central horseshoe-shaped road called

From paintings of Wandjina figures on bark to mass-produced T-shirts, Waringarri Aboriginal Arts shop in Kununurra has the full range of Kimberley commercial Aboriginal art forms. Catering to an ever-growing market for Aboriginal arts and handicrafts, Waringarri and similar shops in Broome and outside Derby are operated by local Aboriginal communities, each favouring the work of local artists.

Coolibah Drive. The ends of the horseshoe join the Ivanhoe Road, which goes out to the farms of the Ord River Project. Most of the shops and offices are within a block of the southern side of Coolibah Drive and radial roads lead off to the residential streets.

Inevitably, Kununurra is modern. In fact, the sight of so many new buildings and numerous conventional suburban houses seems quite incongruous in the Kimberley.

The town's central position in Kimberley affairs makes it an ideal base for exploring the Kimberley, and several hotels, motels and caravan parks have arisen to service that need. From here one can take a conventional plane, float plane, helicopter or 4WD trip down to Bungle Bungle Range, visit Lake Argyle, the irrigation area or Wyndham, or head down the Gibb River Road. Kununurra also has the regional headquarters of the Department of Conservation and Land Management (CALM), which administers all the

national parks of the Kimberley. Its closest charge is Hidden Valley, only a few hundred metres from the westernmost buildings of the township.

The top of Kellys Knob, north of the built-up area, provides an excellent view of the township and the patchwork fields of the irrigation scheme. Throughout the hot days of the tourist season, black kites can be seen soaring along the ridge top within metres of the lookout.

Despite its features, facilities and convenient location, many visitors find Kununurra a jarring element in the Kimberley landscape. There is no feel of a frontier town here, of a place that grew up on adversity and became strong through self-reliance. Rather, it feels too much like the rest of Australia, like just another country town. But that is also Kununurra's main attraction. It's a place in which to shop and rest and it provides a touchstone of normalcy that makes one realise how special the Kimberley is and how unique its other towns really are. **DMcG**.

Sunlight reflecting from water lying on irrigated fields on Ivanhoe Plain highlights the two elements that gave rise to the Ord River Irrigation Project and the township of Kununurra: the fertile black soil (Cununurra clay) and red alluvial sandy loam river plains of the Ord River needed only a regular supply of water to be fertile. However, it has taken about half a century to find a good balance of suitable crops to make the project profitable.

National Parks

The Kimberley is an area of scenic splendour that is uniquely Australian. Here boabs and eucalypts, spinifex-littered buttes and mangrove-lined tidal inlets combine into one fascinating whole. However, the Kimberley came late to the national park scene. Indeed, Australia's first national park, the Royal (just south of Sydney), was proclaimed in April 1879, some three months before Alexander Forrest became the first white person to travel deeply into the interior of the Kimberley.

Six of the seven national parks of the Kimberley give visitors a good cross-section of the interior of the region. The other, Drysdale River National Park, is also situated inland but access is extremely difficult.

With over 25,000 visitors a year, Geikie Gorge is the most popular Kimberley national park, but it is the newest one, Purnululu (Bungle Bungle), that has captured the public imagination. Many visitors are content to see it from the air (on flights from Kununurra, Wyndham and Halls Creek) because the track to the Bungle Bungle Range remains a challenging 4WD experience. The other parks each have their own special appeal: Windjana Gorge and Tunnel Creek (which, with Geikie, are called the "devonian reefs national parks" – see page 14), Hidden Valley and Wolfe Creek Crater.

Every visitor to the Kimberley should seek out as many of the national parks as possible. On a Kimberley map, "National Park" is the designation of an area of special interest – something that stands out even in a region full of geographical oddities and wonderful scenery.

Purnululu (Bungle Bungle)

Purnululu (Bungle Bungle) was declared a National Park in March 1987. No name had been gazetted at the time of writing but the title above is the name CALM has suggested. The park

Mysterious and surreal, the eroded sandstone ridges and domes of the Bungle Bungle Range rise from the flood plains of the Ord River to cover 450 sq. km with hills riddled with creek beds and gorges.

Forming the apt acronym CALM, Western Australia's Department of Conservation and Land Management administers all the national parks of the Kimberley region through its regional headquarters in Kununurra.

covers an area of 210,000 ha with an adjoining 110,000 ha of "conservation reserve" that is largely inaccessible. The feature everyone comes to see is a sandstone massif about 33 km long, 23 km wide and rising to 270 m above the plains. A description of how the Bungle Bungle Range was formed is in "An Ancient Land" on page 25.

It has been suggested that this park has the potential to attract as many visitors as Australia's most famous symbol of the outback, Uluru (Ayers Rock). Although the Bungle Bungle Range doesn't have the same solitary grandeur, it does provide an area of endless fascination: narrow gorges lined with tall *Livistona* palms, occasional isolated pools of water glowing golden in the sunlight reflected from rock walls, and everywhere

the characteristic black-and-orange domes.

We'll probably never know when the first people came to this area. However, archaeologists have unearthed relics from 21,000 years ago downstream on the Ord River. It's likely that settlement was much earlier than that – perhaps as far back as 50,000 years. Certainly the Bungle Bungle Range was a significant feature for several Aboriginal groups at the time when the first white settlers arrived: the massif is destined to prove a cultural treasure-trove of rock paintings and burial sites when a thorough archaeological exploration is carried out.

The first Europeans to see the Bungle Bungle Range were Alexander Forrest and his party in 1879. Looking towards the range, Forrest wrote: "To the north there was nothing promising, all rough and rangy." This opinion carried through to the next century of occupation: no matter how beautiful the spectacle, if cattle couldn't graze on it, the land was worthless.

"Stumpy" Michael Durack, later a partner in nearby Lissadell station, was the first person to take out a lease that covered part of the Bungle Bungle massif. That was in 1881, but this lease lapsed in 1897. The unusual name was probably given to it by Arthur Muggleton, who leased it and nearby Tickalara station between 1929 and 1937. The name may have just been a product of Muggleton's whimsical humour, or it may have been a corruption of "Purnululu", the Aboriginal name for the massif, which simply means "sandstone".

"Bungle Bungle station" subsequently became an outstation of Turner station and, after the Ord River was dammed in 1962, it was included in an area resumed as a regeneration reserve to rectify the results of previous overgrazing.

The area's current high profile came about after the Western Australian Department of Tourism assigned Roger Garwood, a Perth photographer, to photograph it in 1981. Two years later the Bungle Bungle Range featured in the *Wonders of WA* television series. In the 1987 dry season, about 5000 people drove to the massif and 15,500 flew over it.

Reaching towards the sun, a group of young palm trees fills the floor of a canyon in the Bungle Bungle Range. Some of the plants in the region of the Bungle Bungle massif have been discovered by botanists so recently that they have yet to be named. On the massif itself, the most pervasive and spectacular is this unnamed species of Livistona *fan palm.*

A gallery of ochre-outlined hand stencils near a creek bed within the Bungle Bungle Range reflects the long association between Aborigines and the valleys of the massif. The age of the paintings ranges from ancient to relatively recent: some of the children's hand-prints found here were made by adults now living in local communities and townships.

An Aboriginal legend tells of a galah fighting with an echidna. As the galah attacked, the echidna frantically dug holes in an attempt to hide, thus forming the mounds and hollows of the Bungle Bungle Range. Finally, the echidna raised its quills to fend off the attacker but they all fell out. Those quills became the tall palm trees scattered about the Bungle Bungle massif.

All tourist activity is restricted to the western and southern sides of the massif – the only parts accessible from the track that comes in from the Great Northern Highway. The western part is an area of tall cliffs and narrow gorges (such as Echidna Chasm), while the southern end, along Piccaninny Creek, has the banded domes for which the Bungle Bungle Range is famous. From the air, the most clearly distinguishable single feature is Piccaninny Gorge: a deep gash that almost cuts the main massif in two.

Geikie Gorge

When you travel by boat along the Fitzroy River where it crosses the Geikie Range, the most striking feature you see is the bands of colour in the rock in the gorge. It's like a layer cake: the rock directly above the river is a pale cream; above 15 m there is a distinct shift to an orange/grey, which extends skywards.The demarcation is the floodline, the height the water reaches when the Fitzroy changes from the sluggish stream of the dry season into the raging torrent of the Wet, draining an area half the size of Victoria at

Testimony to the power of floodwaters, the walls of Geikie Gorge are bleached to heights of 15 m above the dry season river level. The peak flow of the Fitzroy in flood is a remarkable 29,800 cu. m a second.

Plying the calm waters of the Fitzroy River through Geikie Gorge, the regular CALM ranger-conducted tours introduce more than 25,000 visitors each year to basking fresh-water crocodiles, sleeping fruit bats in riverside trees and a wide range of plant life. It is only possible to see the gorge from the river: to protect plant and animal life along the river banks during the dry season, visitors are not allowed within 200 m of the river on either bank except at one point near the public camping area.

a rate of 29,800 cubic metres per second. In the Wet, the camping ground of the 3000 ha park doesn't host visitors: it is seven metres under water.

From the air, the Geikie Range still looks quite a lot like the offshore reef it was 350 million years ago when it formed around the island that is now the Mitchell Plateau. The 6 km long gorge was formed as the Fitzroy River cut through the soft limestone (see "An Ancient Land" on page 13). The effect today is spectacular: this special combination of river and rock (and the area's many birds, fish and crocodiles) attracts thousands of visitors every year.

Some of the fish found in the river hark back to the region's oceanic origins. Swordfish and stingrays, normally saltwater creatures, are sometimes found in the Fitzroy River at Geikie Gorge, more than 300 km from the coast. They have fully adapted to fresh water and live alongside the more typical river dwellers of the Kimberley: barramundi and freshwater crocodiles.

Geikie Gorge was named "Geikie Canyon" by Edward T. Hardman, the WA Government Geologist, in 1883 in honour of the noted British geologist, Sir Archibald Geikie. It was a most fitting piece of nomenclature, considering the special geological features of the park.

Wolfe Creek Crater

About 250,000 years ago, a lump of cosmic iron (which may have weighed up to 50,000 tonnes) collided with the Earth 150 km south of the present township of Halls Creek. This was no mere shooting star, disintegrating on contact with the atmosphere in a brief flash of fire. Our atmosphere hardly slowed this meteorite down at all – it probably hit the ground at a speed of 100,000 km/h or more!

The crater left by the impact is almost one kilometre across and initially may have been over 150 m deep. It has since been largely filled by shifting desert sands and today the rim is only 50 m above the interior and about 30 m above the surrounding desert. Indeed, only low rainfall and very slow erosion have allowed the crater to remain so clearly recognisable.

The best perspective of the crater is obtained from the air: it appears as an enormous pock-mark in the arid plain. Although the unusual formation had been noted by people on the ground, it was only after Dr Frank Reeves, a geologist, flew over the crater in June 1947 and later returned on a land expedition that the theory that it is a meteorite crater was widely accepted (although some geologists still believe it to be of volcanic origin).

In fact, the Wolfe Creek Meteorite Crater is regarded as the second largest meteorite crater on Earth – after the much more recently formed Coon Butte Crater near Canyon Diablo in the North American State of Arizona, which is 1.6 km wide. Wolfe Creek itself is a small stream east of the 1460 ha park, which was named after Robert Tennant Stowe Wolfe (not "Wolf" as it is often wrongly spelt), an early prospector in the region.

Windjana Gorge

Like Geikie Gorge, Windjana Gorge is a cleft through a fossil reef. However, the Lennard River flows through Windjana Gorge only in the wet season: in the Dry, it's a series of deep, cool pools at the foot of high orange-grey cliffs. These cliffs, with deep grooves between the columns of limestone, give the impression of organ pipes. This effect has come about through the weathering of the limestone by small streams of water

A one-kilometre-wide bullseye in the desert, Wolfe Creek Meteorite Crater, the second largest confirmed crater in the world, was formed 250,000 years ago when a 50,000-tonne body struck at 100,000 km/h. (The largest such formation is 1.6 km wide Coon Butte Crater in Arizona.) Wolfe Creek Meteorite Crater has retained its symmetry well because of the dry desert conditions.

(Top) A series of ponds under clear blue skies in the dry season, the Lennard River gives no indication of its wet season force which has cut 4 km through the Napier Range to create 90 m high cliffs.

(Below) A damp, dark place inhabited by bats, Tunnel Creek is made less daunting by a roof collapse that has created a natural skylight. The creek began as a fault line in the limestone of the Napier Range. Over the millennia, water dissolved the rock to form the underground creek.

(Far right) Grooves worn by Aborigines sharpening spears and axes point to the heart of Hidden Valley. This national park is only a few minutes' walk from Kununurra but its boab trees and lilies, weathered sandstone domes and Aboriginal carving provide a microcosm of the Kimberley.

that have been sufficiently acidic to dissolve the chemically sensitive limestone.

Lush vegetation, including figs and river red gums, lines the banks of the river at the base of the cliffs but the top of the ridges have only sparse vegetation, principally tussock grass. There are generally harmless freshwater crocodiles living in the pools, along with a large fish population. The fish are the attraction for the numerous waterbirds that live in the 2134 ha park during the Dry. These include herons and the large, stately jabiru. There are Aboriginal rock paintings here, and for many Kimberley visitors this will be the only chance to see Wandjina figures, those enigmatic faces from the Dreaming in their true setting.

Tunnel Creek

Down the track between Windjana and Geikie gorges lies Tunnel Creek. Under the harsh tropical sun that scorches the Kimberley, Tunnel Creek is a very special place. For this is a cold, damp walk along a path under a limestone ridge. In some places, the 750 m path is dark and a torch is required. However, in the middle of the underground walkway is a bright place where sunlight streams through a hole in the roof of the cave. This is the result of the limestone roof collapsing after being undermined by the river. Tunnel Creek has taken the easiest path in its course along a fault line through the limestone. The most notable inhabitants of this 91 ha park are the several species of bats that have taken up residence in the underground caverns.

Hidden Valley

Not everyone has the chance to explore Purnululu (Bungle Bungle) on foot. However, there is an easily accessible alternative that, while not

so extensive or impressive as that wonderland, still gives a feeling for the banded sandstone towers of the Kimberley. Hidden Valley is less than five minutes by car from the centre of Kununurra, yet within the narrow gorges of the 1817 ha park the only signs of civilisation are the graded tracks and picnic facilities.

There are several boabs near the road within Hidden Valley. The more enthusiastic visitor can climb to the top of the ridge past the end of the road for a bird's-eye view over the northern part of Kununurra. Perhaps more rewarding is the path to the right near the entrance to the park. This leads down to a picturesque lily pond that is a natural rock pool. Hidden Valley is either a tantalising preview of what is awaiting in the Kimberley or a final chance to absorb the atmosphere that makes the region so appealing.

Drysdale River

There is no access road into Drysdale River National Park, a vast 435,906 ha wilderness in the north Kimberley. Indeed, even the park administrators knew little about it until a 1975 scientific expedition surveyed it and noted a great diversity of life including 594 different plants and some 2500 animal species. It looks set to remain an almost untouched example of the Kimberley

landscape: a place of eucalyptus forests and densely vegetated riverbanks and billabongs.

DMcG.

Wildlife

There is no doubt that scenery, wildlife and Aboriginal culture are the Kimberley's main tourist attractions. It's impossible to travel through the region without being impressed by the variety of native animals one sees.

Most notable are the birds. In fact, dawn at the Marlgu Billabong (outside Wyndham) can be the most memorable experience of a northern holiday. Here countless wildfowl are concentrated into quite a small area. Herons, black swans, pelicans, ibis, stilts, jabiru, spoonbills, cranes and many varieties of ducks are just part of the passing parade. At this billabong, and at other waterholes, one may chance upon brolgas performing a mating dance that has much of the grace and elegance of a courtly quadrille.

There are some species of northern birds that impress by their sheer numbers. In the dry season, when burning off is common, every swirling column of smoke is full of black kites feeding on the insects borne aloft on the thermal currents. Flocks of budgerigars sweep across the road in the drier grasslands, then disappear in an iridescent green flash when their passage is interrupted by a car. Often trees appear to have erupted in dense clumps of large white blooms, which closer inspection reveals to be sulphur-crested cockatoos or corellas. (Black cockatoos are common, too, although not seen in such large flocks.) But the Kununurra sky darkened by an endless stream of magpie geese is the Kimberley's most imposing wildlife sight.

Rivers in the Kimberley are full of fish. Small black bream appear to be in every permanent waterhole in the north. The common insect-eating archer fish shoots water from its mouth to knock prey off overhanging branches.

The mammals and reptiles of the Kimberley are generally quite elusive, but wallaroos and several species of wallaby may be seen; trees near water can be festooned with flying foxes during the day; snakes, frill-necked lizards, marsupial mice and bandicoots are present but shy. New species of reptiles are still being discovered in the Kimberley. An emu or dingo may be seen on rare occasions. **DMcG.**

Disturbed by the photographer, a goanna near Derby extends its tongue to scent the intruder and keeps a wary eye on him. Goannas (of which there are 35 species worldwide – 24 in Australia) are Australia's largest lizards. The family name is a corruption of "iguana", a completely different family. Goannas are non-venomous and, despite displays of bravado, not dangerous.

(Centre) Still, but perfectly co-ordinated, a pair of brolgas stand in the shallows of Marlgu Billabong. Brolgas grow to 1.5 m high, making them one of the continent's largest bird species. Pairs frequently "dance" with remarkable grace.

(Far left) Filling the sky, a flock of hardhead ducks flies from Marlgu Billabong. The hardhead flies faster than most ducks and can remain under water for periods of up to one minute.

Crocodiles

Clutching a flower between its teeth, a baby freshwater crocodile is surrounded by the pioneers of a new Australian industry: crocodile farming. Besides bringing commercial gains from both tourism and crocodile products, crocodile farming is adding considerably to our knowledge of this creature, whose ancestors survived for over 200 million years with little change. In this farm at Broome, these young crocodiles face a much better chance of reaching adulthood than those born in the wild, where less than 1 per cent of eggs result in mature crocodiles.

In May 1987, the Kimberley came under the world media spotlight when a visiting American model was taken by a crocodile near waterfalls on the Prince Regent River. This certainly highlighted the danger of approaching the Kimberley's most exotic inhabitant.

"All crocs are territorial," Malcolm Douglas told me as we walked around his crocodile park in Broome. "But each has a distinct personality and some are more aggressive about it than others.

"Now Agro here won't take any encroachment lightly." Malcolm had a long wooden pole in his hand that he extended over the fence and across the placid waters of a pool. "Look what happens when I just touch the surface lightly." The pool instantly exploded in a thrashing frenzy, a seething mass of water and glistening ridges and teeth. It was my first real insight into what the last minutes of those who had gambled on swimming in crocodile-inhabited waters, and lost, must have been like.

There are two species of Australian crocodile: "salties" and "freshies". The freshwater crocodile *(Crocodylus johnstoni)* is almost universally regarded as harmless. It's certainly quite timid in

the wild. Not so *Crocodylus porosus*, which grows much larger than the freshie and is quite ready to regard people as a meal. Some authorities encourage the use of the term "estuarine" rather than "saltwater" crocodile as this species can be found in fresh water 100 km or more inland. The two types are easily distinguished: a freshie has a much finer snout and, less obviously, a row of four large plates on the neck, immediately below the head.

Crocodiles are reptiles that have existed for some 200 million years; they are found through-out northern Australia, from Broome on the Kimberley coast to Rockhampton on the eastern coast of Queensland. During the late 1970s and early '80s there was heated debate about their numbers and whether we needed to be protected from them, or vice versa. Freshwater crocodiles have been protected in WA since 1962 and salties since 1970 (in both cases WA set the lead for other States) and the export of skins was pro-hibited by federal law in 1972. A rapid increase in tourism in the north and an increase in the number of saltwater crocodiles has increased the

Holding one of his new-born charges, adventurer and film-maker turned Kimberley crocodile farmer Malcolm Douglas shows how hatchlings are perfect crocodiles in miniature; every plate and feature is in perfect detail. The sex of a crocodile is determined by the temperature at which the egg is kept. If it varies much above or below 32°C, the crocodile will be female; a constant 32°C will produce a male.

Lashing the pool in a frenzy, a large saltwater crocodile at Broome Crocodile Park shows his displeasure when the keeper touches the water with a pole. Crocodiles are extremely territorial and any intrusion may be greeted by attack.

potential for tragedy. The best advice is: if a local resident or a sign says "don't swim", don't. Nor should anyone consider stealing crocodile warning signs – doing so can be tantamount to manslaughter.

The growing number of crocodile farms in WA, the NT and Queensland is a response to Australian saltwater crocodiles being transferred from Appendix 1 to Appendix 2 of the CITES agreement. CITES is the Convention on International Trade in Endangered Species of Wild Flora and Fauna. The more flexible Appendix 2 allows limited

commercial use of wild stocks under close scrutiny. Besides providing handbags, shoes and steaks, the crocodile farms provide a useful base for scientific research and close, safe access to crocodiles for tourists.

Still, there is nothing like the thrill of seeing your first crocodile in the wild – from a safe vantage point. As a fisherman on the Wyndham wharf told me: "Everyone comes up here and they all want to see crocodiles. A few find out that the only thing worse than not seeing a croc while you're here is meeting one unexpectedly." **DMcG**.

Daunting in their saw-blade array, the teeth of this mature saltwater crocodile are ideally suited to a diet mainly of mud crabs, turtles and, occasionally, birds and mammals. The teeth of a freshwater crocodile are finer, in keeping with their smaller prey. Crocodiles require food only once a week and have small stomachs: keeping the rest for a later meal rather than a preference for rotting meat is the reason crocodiles stow meat under water.

Barramundi

The opportunity to fish for barramundi is a lure for visitors to the Kimberley. It's high on the locals' list of sports, too. Barramundi is one of the world's great game and table fish, providing both a thrill in the catching and excellent eating. Like the estuarine crocodile, it is found throughout northern Australia from the Ashburton River, WA to the Mary River, Queensland. Southern anglers must travel north to experience the excitement of catching "barra".

Tales of "barra" weighing in at up to 50 kg are legion, though a 1970s tagging survey in the NT found an average weight of 2.6 kg. Fishing expert Steve Starling says that amateurs should regard any barramundi over 8 kg as noteworthy and a catch over 20 kg as only an outside chance. The most popular fishing spots are along the Fitzroy River near Derby and the Ord River near Kununurra (especially at Ivanhoe Crossing).

Remote, rarely fished areas may yield larger fish. However, its unusual life cycle makes it highly vulnerable to overfishing.

The barramundi is highly adapted to the climate and seasons of tropical Australia. Between October and January barramundi make their way to the sea to spawn. The larvae develop into small fish in the salt water and then make their way up the river systems until the streams stop flowing. Obviously, high dam walls block this migratory path but, where possible, the fish may proceed farther upstream in the next Wet. At age three or four, they all mature as males and make their first return journey to the sea to spawn. Between the ages of six and eight some become female in a process called protandry. As all female barramundi are large, overfishing is a real threat.

The Fisheries Department of WA (with an office in Broome) is developing a plan to avoid this. A licence is not required for barramundi but there's a limit of five "barra" per person per day. **DMcG.**

A solitary fisherman tries for a last catch at Ivanhoe Crossing, 8 km from Kununurra. A popular fishing spot, Ivanhoe Crossing is the first obstacle barramundi meet on their way up the Ord River and they must wait until enough water flows over the crossing to allow them to continue.

Kununurra resident Bill Treasure catches a barramundi below the dam gates of Lake Kununurra. His verdict was that it was too small, so it was unhooked and released back into the river. Pelicans in the background, unhindered by bag limits, successfully fished throughout the afternoon. Barramundi are particularly prone to overfishing. There are no female barramundi less than six years old so catching large fish takes a disproportionate percentage of females, reducing breeding potential.

Podaxis sp. *(podaxis fungus)*

(Left) Livistona sp. – *undescribed fan palm*

Rhizophora stylosa *(stilt-rooted mangrove)*

Banksia dentata *(tropical banksia)*

Plants of the

Calytrix
exstipulata
(turkey bush)

Acacia tumida *(pindan wattle)*

Cycas basaltica *(cycad, female)*

Eucalyptus miniata *(woollybutt)*

Kimberley

Gyrocarpus americanus *(helicopter tree) fruits*

Grevillea pyramidalis *(caustic bush)*

Calandrinia sp.
(parakeelya)

Boabs

Boabs are your constant companions in the Kimberley; silvery giants with huge trunks and stubby branches growing in a cluster from the top. Their expressive postures make it hard not to humanise boab trees – particularly when there are a couple of bulky parent trees surrounded by a brood of skinny offspring.

In Australia the boab is found only in the Kimberley and a neighbouring area of the NT. It is the sole representative here of the genus *Adansonia*. There are nine species in the genus, seven of which are found only on the island of Madagascar, off the east coast of Africa. The baobab or monkey-bread tree (*Adansonia digitata*) is widespread in tropical Africa. Most probably, boabs and baobabs were neighbours when the continents were joined together as Pangaea. However, another theory suggests that both species came from Madagascar around 190 million years ago, after nuts were swept across the ocean and deposited on these distant shores.

The name "boab" is a truncation of the African name for its species: "baobab". Indeed, the *Macquarie Dictionary* gives "baobab" as the preferred spelling. However, in the Kimberley the Australian variant is universally used.

(Far left) *Covered in graffiti and fenced off, the "Prison Tree" near Derby is different from the way it must have appeared when it was a landmark in the wilderness on the approach to Derby. There is no recorded case of this or the other "prison tree" near Wyndham being used to contain prisoners, but they may have been chained to the base of the tree.*

(Left) *Strange single or multiple bulbous forms are a characteristic of the boab tree, so it's not surprising it came to be known as the "bottle tree". Australian boabs don't grow as tall as African baobabs but can develop a larger circumference – of up to 16 m.*

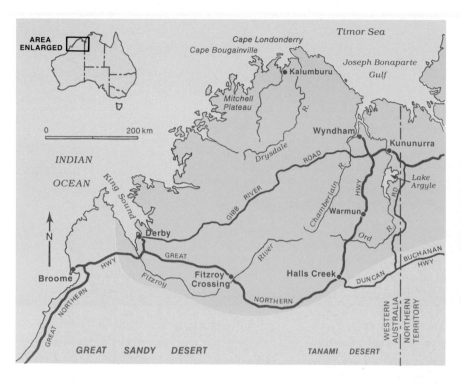

(Above) The natural distribution of boabs in the Kimberley.

The botanical name of the boab is *Adansonia gregorii*, named after the noted explorer Augustus Gregory. The tree was first described in 1857 from specimens obtained by the botanist Ferdinand von Mueller on the Augustus Gregory expedition of 1855.

Today the photographers who bewail the difficulty of finding a roadside boab that hasn't been defaced by graffiti carved into the bark may not realise this is the continuation of a long-standing tradition. The first European to describe the tree was Phillip Parker King, who referred to "the gouty habit of the stem". His crew carved "H.M.C. MERMAID 1820" on a boab near the mouth of the Prince Regent River. Thirty-five years later, Augustus Gregory carved a message

for following members of his party into a boab on the banks of the Victoria River.

The boab flower is creamy white and about 10 cm long. The large fruit (up to 25 cm long and 15 cm in diameter) is initially green and hairy but becomes brown and furry. Inside, dozens of black seeds are packed into the pulp. The boab is deciduous, losing its leaves in the dry season to retain moisture stored in the soft, spongy wood.

Boabs grow quickly and may live for more than 1000 years – one in Africa is estimated to be 5000 years old! These enormous trees can have a circumference greater than their height. Folklore says that boabs near Wyndham and Derby were used as overnight cells by police officers transporting prisoners. However, prisoners were probably chained to, not put inside, the trees.

Kimberley Aborigines used the boab as an all-purpose provider. The pith of the seed is edible (with high protein and vitamin C content) and was sometimes crushed to a powder and made into a bread. Moisture can be extracted from the wood or roots, the gum makes a convenient glue and the bark can be used as twine.

These days, boab nuts serve mainly as artists' canvases sold as souvenirs, especially around Wyndham, where every store seems to carry them. The smooth, brown fur of the nuts is carved, with varying degrees of skill, by Kimberley artists.

Probably the best place to see a large collection of boab trees of all shapes and sizes is at Derby airport. With their grotesque limbs and distended trunks silhouetted against the setting sun, they remind one of Ernestine Hill's description of the boab in *The Great Australian Loneliness*: "A Caliban of a tree, a grizzled, distorted old goblin – a friendly ogre of the great North-west". **DMcG.**

Etched into the brown, velvet-textured surface of boab nuts, scenes of outback life take on an extra dimension. As it matures, the boab fruit changes from green and hairy to a brown, woody shell that becomes the artist's canvas. Inside are scores of hard, black seeds in a firm, pithy matrix.

The Back of Beyond

Protruding above a mass of greenery on the red soil at the northern tip of Dampier Land, Cape Leveque lighthouse marks the western entrance to King Sound. It is accessible by road, sea or air. It's about 16 km from both Lombardina Mission to the south and the pearl farm at One Arm Point. The 195 km drive from Broome to Cape Leveque is over rough, unformed, sandy roads that soon become impassable in wet weather.

From the security of Australia's large cities and the well-developed areas of the east coast, the whole of the remote, empty Kimberley seems like a wilderness. However, the truth is that some of the Kimberley is generally as readily accessible as anywhere else in Australia. The towns of Broome, Derby, Fitzroy Crossing, Halls Creek, Wyndham and Kununurra are all linked by an all-weather road and one can travel right across the Kimberley without difficulty.

There are some areas of the Kimberley, however, that are only seen by the most intrepid traveller. The adventure of getting to these places is just as important as the destination itself.

The "alternative route" across the Kimberley is the 700 km of the "Gibb River Road" between Derby and Wyndham. The Gibb River Road is, in fact, two roads: the Derby–Gibb River and the Gibb River–Wyndham roads. The whole route cuts through the heart of the Kimberley; after the first 68 km of sealed road out of

Derby it is unsealed (but well formed enough for road trains) right through until it rejoins the highway, 48 km out of Wyndham. Between November and March, you should check with the police at either end before setting out, as rain can swell the creeks and make the road impassable. As with any form of travel off the highway in the Kimberley, motorists should ensure they have spare tyres and parts as well as food and water enough to last through any emergency. Fuel requirement calculations should be pessimistic enough to account for some rough, slow going.

After turning off onto the Gibb River Road, one continues across the coastal plains before climbing onto the uplands of the central Kimberley. The turnoff to Windjana Gorge and Tunnel Creek is 126 km from Derby – that road will eventually bring you back onto the highway 42 km west of Fitzroy Crossing. Straight ahead, some supplies, fuel and camping are available at Mt Barnett station (313 km). There is accommodation at Mt

Detailing points of interest along the "Gibb River Road" and beyond, a sign outside Derby puts much of the Kimberley in perspective. Constructed to open up the heart of the Kimberley and facilitate cattle movement, this alternative route extends for 700 km between Derby and Wyndham. Although the all-weather Great Northern Highway is 230 km longer, that is the much faster route.

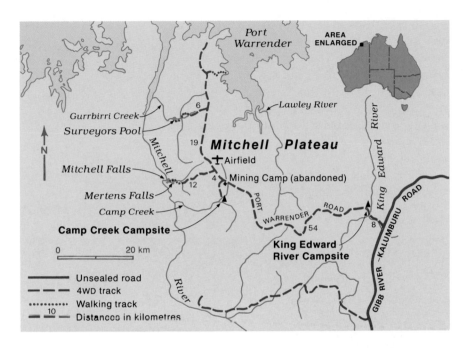

Port
Warrender

AREA
ENLARGED

Lawley River

Gurrbirri Creek
Surveyors Pool

6

19 **Mitchell Plateau**
✝ Airfield

King Edward River

Mitchell Falls

12 4 Mining Camp (abandoned)

Mertens Falls

Camp Creek

Camp Creek Campsite

0   20 km

PORT

WARRENDER ROAD

54

8

King Edward
River Campsite

GIBB RIVER – KALUMBURU ROAD

Mitchell

River

Unsealed road
4WD track
Walking track
10 Distances in kilometres

N

(Above) The tracks of the Mitchell Plateau provide the best chance to explore remote parts of the Kimberley. (Left) Plunging over the edge of the Mitchell Plateau in a series of giant cascades and pools, the Mitchell River creates Mitchell Falls. The river was named after Sir James Mitchell, Premier of Western Australia. The falls and plateau were named much later and took their names from the river.

Elizabeth station (345 km) and permanent water but no camping at Campbell Creek (461 km), Dawn Creek (484 km) and the Durack River (505 km). "Karunjie" station (turn at 510 km, it's officially still known as Pentecost Downs station) is 48 km down a rough track and visitors are welcome to stay (and meals and tours are provided) if prior arrangements are made.

Dawn at the place known as Jacks Waterhole (533 km) is a wonderful time of day. Near the store is a camping ground next to a large billabong. Facilities and services include fuel, toilets, hot showers and cold drinks. At first light, a pair of brolgas that have taken up residence here can often be seen dancing and there are myriad other birds on hand even if the brolgas are not in attendance. The owners charge a daily entrance fee to the area and guided tours of the surrounding district in their 4WD are available.

At the 586 km mark you reach the top of the Pentecost Range and 2 km farther along there are spectacular views of the flat mesas of the Cockburn Range and down into Cambridge Gulf. Home Valley station (591 km – then it's one km down the fork to the left) is leased by the Sinnamon family who also run Jacks Waterhole and "Karunjie". It also has an admission fee that gives access to the same facilities as at Jacks Waterhole. Fuel and a telephone are also available. Nine kilometres from Home Valley the road crosses the Pentecost River. Despite the tempting expanse of cool water, the river is tidal here and home to saltwater crocodiles, so it's not for swimming. There is camping and drinking water at "Fish Hole" (620 km) and El Questro station (18 km to the right at 624 km). From here it is only 34 km to the Great Northern Highway and Wyndham 48 km farther north.

About 315 km from Derby and 40 km past Gibb River station lies the turn-off onto the Kalumburu–Mitchell Plateau Road. Permission must be obtained from the community at Kalumburu before going there and accommodation must be arranged in advance through the monastery. Permission is not automatically granted but, if it is, the effort is well worthwhile. The old mission buildings, with the well-kept orchards and gardens behind, are beautiful and there is a lot of good fishing in the area. On the other side of the airstrip are the wrecks of some aircraft destroyed in Japanese air raids during World War II. The large wartime "Truscott" US air base lies some 20 km to the north but it is now almost completely overgrown and only a large collection of abandoned 44-gallon drums of stale fuel marks the site. Kalumburu is 270 km from the Gibb River Road. It takes several weeks after the end of the Wet for the road, which was only surveyed in 1955, to be graded and reopened.

About 163 km along the Kalumburu Road is the turn-off to the Mitchell Plateau, which may soon be declared a national park. William Easton, who led a government expedition across the plateau in 1921, named the river after Sir James Mitchell, a Premier of WA. When extensive bauxite deposits were discovered there in 1965 by a mineral company's exploration team, expedition leader Ken Malcolm named the plateau after the adjoining river.

The track onto the Mitchell Plateau is definitely for 4WD vehicles only. There is a good riverside campsite (which is very popular and can be crowded but it does have permanent fresh water) about two kilometres on the right after you cross the King Edward River. About half a kilometre past the mining camp, 57 km along the track, there is a turn-off to the left that leads to Camp Creek, 8 km ahead in an open valley. This is a popular camp base for exploring the other features of the plateau. Four and a half kilometres north of the mining camp is the turn-off to Mitchell Falls – you can drive to Mertens Creek, 12 km from the turn-off and there is a 45-minute walk to the falls. The trail is marked by yellow discs. Allow extra time to relax at the falls. Although there is camping here, sites are limited. Camp Creek is a better option.

The last major side feature on the way to Walsh Point and the termination of the road at the edge of Port Warrender is the Surveyors Pool, surrounded by white cliffs of King Leopold sandstone. If you are thinking of camping here, bear in mind that no water is available on the walk in, although water-bottles can be filled at the pool and carried out. The turn-off to the Surveyors Pool is 24 km after the mining camp – you can drive 6 km but must walk the last 4 km.

Many of the best sights in the Kimberley can only be explored from the water or seen from the air. I found a special highlight of the Kimberley was the Elgee Cliffs along the western bank of the Chamberlain River. Although these run parallel with the Great Northern Highway for about 125 km (the road is at least 50 km to the east), they are hidden by intervening ranges and can be seen and fully appreciated only from the air. Imagine a very straight river stretching to the horizon with a high steep bank rising along its length to the

Sister Scholastica, seen here riding past the chapel on the mission's motor-tricycle, is a regular sight around the Kalumburu community, the northernmost settlement in WA. With Kalumburu's large vegetable garden and extensive community, the "trike" is invaluable as an all-purpose, lightweight vehicle. The first Catholic mission in the area was established in 1908. It shifted to Kalumburu in the 1930s. The community is accessible by road or aircraft. To the north, the ruined "Truscott", a World War II air base, is recognisable by the abandoned fuel drums and overgrown runway.

sharply defined angle of the crest. That's the view of Elgee Cliffs from an aircraft flying at about 5000 feet. Even among the considerable scenic grandeur of the rest of the Kimberley, these cliffs stand out. Nearby El Questro station, nestled in the valley, looks very much like paradise – it certainly has a very dramatic backdrop.

A flight along the Kimberley coast serves as an incentive to explore the area fully by boat. North of Broome, the Dampier Land peninsula has kilometre after kilometre of empty beaches only accessible from the sea or by 4WD along a narrow coastal track. The main road through the middle of the peninsula lea 's over monotonous plains to the Beagle Bay Mission. The interior of the mission's church is fabulous. It is set with pearl shell and there is an intricacy of design and an ornate richness that contrasts with the often starkly practical image of the Kimberley. Beyond Beagle Bay is the community at Lombadina and the cultured pearl farm at Cygnet Bay. At Cape Leveque stands a lighthouse and not far away is

Abseiling into a 30 m crevasse, a mining engineer completes a training exercise in the Mimbi Creek gorge in the Lawford Range, 100 km east of Fitzroy Crossing. This course, conducted by Adventure West for the Chamber of Mines and Energy of Western Australia, is aimed at developing self-sufficiency in remote situations and an appreciation of the environment. This area is on a private pastoral lease and not marked on any tourist map.

the community at One Arm Point.

As you fly north from Derby, the mudflats of King Sound give way to the wonderfully picturesque islands of the Buccaneer Archipelago. Even the iron ore islands of Cockatoo and Koolan add to the spectacle. The few buildings of Cockatoo Island run along the narrow central spine; and the gaping open cut of Koolan Island is right next to the wharf accommodating large ore-carrying vessels. On the ebb or flood of the tide, the nearby tidal races of "The Gaps" or The Funnel present an astounding picture. At each,

huge volumes of water flow into and out of a large bay through a channel only a few metres wide. Even in more open waters there are eddies and races as the water seeks base level.

Walcott Inlet is an appealing bay that would be well settled if it were almost anywhere else on Earth. In the Kimberley, it's a getaway destination for enthusiastic fishermen, although there has been a proposal put forward to develop the site as an exclusive retreat. Farther north, Kuri Bay is by far the largest pearl farm on the Kimberley coast and east of it is the Prince Regent

River, looking too straight to be natural, particularly with both the river and its numerous tributaries flowing along fault lines to join at right angles. The Prince Regent River falls are a stirring sight during the wet season, but few people have seen them then: suitable flying weather is uncertain at this time so the only practical means of access is by boat.

While flying from the Prince Regent River north-east to Kalumburu, strict attention must be paid to navigation. Then, as the north-east coast comes into view, the rivers flow off the eastern side of the plateau in a series of spectacular waterfalls. The few hours' flying time are just sufficient to convince anyone that the only way to return to this spot is with a well-provisioned yacht, a skipper with expertise in tricky conditions, the necessary landing permits from the Aboriginal communities along the coast and at least six months to spare. That's about all one requires to have a chance to fully appreciate the glories of the Kimberley coastline and its hinterland. **DMcG.**

(Far left) Remote and spectacularly beautiful, Cockatoo Island has recently switched from mining to tourism. The old iron ore mine, which closed in 1985, wasn't open to visitors. Redeveloped by Dalhold Investments, a Bond company, it opened in 1989 as a wilderness lodge. It is accessible by air or sea.

Standing in isolation, the 385 m plug of Mt Trafalgar is one of the highest points along the Kimberley coast. On the northern side of the mouth of the Prince Regent River, the massive bluff is a remnant of ancient sandstone beds. Mt Trafalgar can be reached only by boat or helicopter.

"AUSTRALIAN GEOGRAPHIC is looking for a couple who would like to have the experience of their lives by spending a year, virtually isolated, in one of Australia's wild places."
AUSTRALIAN GEOGRAPHIC
Issue 4, October–December 1986

That was how it all began – less than half a page in a journal that would change our lives forever. We were just one of about 500 couples to apply, but fortune smiled on us and we were selected to depart from the populated parts of Australia to live in the sparsely inhabited "Kunmunya Aboriginal Reserve" on the Kimberley coast at Port George IV. The "Kunmunya Mission" itself was abandoned in 1951 and, in our early research before heading out, we learnt that the last of the fully initiated tribal Aboriginal elders of the area had died only the year before.

There was a flurry of activity between being put in the spotlight as "the wilderness couple" at the first AUSTRALIAN GEOGRAPHIC award night and finally setting out. It was all interviews and preparation and trying to anticipate everything that could happen to us in our year in the bush. Inevitably, the events of the wilderness year were far different from what we had envisaged sitting in our home in Fern Tree Gully, Victoria.

In June 1987 we set out on the first leg of our journey to Perth and then up through Derby to Kunmunya. With us we had everything we thought a 20th-century Australian couple would need to survive in the wild. That made a 400 kg pile of food, fishing gear, seeds, tools, books, tents, mosquito nets and a solar/battery-powered radio transmitter. We also had a small dinghy with a 25 hp outboard.

Our backgrounds gave us reason to think that we knew our way around the bush.

Michael was Ranger-in-Charge of Fern Tree Gully National Park; I've lived in the wilderness of Cape Tribulation as part of three months spent exploring the wilderness areas along the north coast, and we've travelled together around Australia several times. However, the battle against the elements that is life in the wilds of the Kimberley was far more of a struggle than we could have imagined.

The events of the year are largely unimpor-

tant; it is the total experience that counts. And now, back home again, I can finally put it in perspective and assess it. It was a fantastic experience that gave us a chance to reassess our lives.

Our year included staying at the camp for a couple of months after the Wet when we finally had a chance to fully explore the land that had been our home for a year. If we had left straight after the Wet (and there were times

when that option was very attractive) our memories would have been negative. But those last two incredible months put the tough times in perspective and we could see them as essential parts of the whole experience.

When Michael and I went to the Kimberley, we had just come together again after a separation. We had known each other most of our lives and were married 15 years earlier when Michael was 23 and I was 20. No one knows what the future holds, but the experiences we shared in the Kimberley have brought us very close together. We have a bond between ourselves and the land on which we lived and this is pretty special. It was essential that we should be able to rely on each other and the result was the strange experience of getting to know someone whom you already know very well.

However, it was definitely an experience in which we grew away from a lot of things that are taken for granted. Although we took a Walkman and some tapes, I only listened to half of one side in the whole year and Michael would have heard just a few hours of music altogether. He preferred to play his guitar. Back home now, we haven't even set the stereo up and only turn the television on if there is something on the ABC we really want to see. I can't tolerate commercials at all now, though in the past they were just something irritating in the background.

At the end of the 12 months in the bush, coming into the town of South Hedland was overwhelming. I know it isn't the big city but we found it hard to accept all the cars and people. Michael left me to do some shopping at an air-

conditioned shopping complex and when he returned I broke into tears and cried: "I can't stand this." By the time we had reached Perth, we were acclimatised to the sights and sounds of civilisation again but we were still very conscious of the intrusive noise of jackhammers and such which no one else seemed to notice.

Most of us have to shut that part of us off which says: "I want to be free, to get back to basics." It's just not practicable to hang onto those ideals in city living. Our time in the Kimberley let us develop that need in ourselves and that was the most important part of the exercise. I don't want to let it go again.

– Susan Cusack

Bringing the tools of civilisation to the bush, Michael and Susan Cusack, AUSTRALIAN GEOGRAPHIC's "Wilderness Couple", stepped ashore near the ruins of Kunmunya mission on Sunday, 28 June 1987. The 9.7 m launch White Shadow *brought the couple up the coast from Derby. Plastic drums of food, metal drums of fuel, mountain bikes, gardening supplies and building tools were unloaded from* White Shadow's *barge onto the rocky shore of what was to be their home for a year.*

Travelling to the Kimberley

By air

There are flights into the main Kimberley towns from Perth and Darwin (and regional centres in between) by the only airline flying into the Kimberley, Ansett WA, a division of Ansett Transport Industries. The Kimberley towns serviced by regular flights are: Kununurra, Derby and Broome.

By car

The distances from Kununurra to the following cities by road are:

Darwin: 870
Perth: 3200
Brisbane: 3500
Sydney: 4300
Melbourne: 3700
Adelaide: 3100

The distance from Broome to Kununurra is 1064 km.

Motoring information is available from the RAC of WA, 228 Adelaide Terrace, Perth, WA 6000.
Tel. (09) 421 4444.

Rental cars

Rental cars are available only in the main towns of the Kimberley: Broome, Derby, Wyndham and Kununurra. In all cases, you have an option of 4WD or conventional vehicle. If you intend to use the vehicle in or near town, a conventional vehicle will be adequate for your needs. It will also be considerably cheaper and consume a lot less petrol.

Tour operators

Land

Tours are conducted in and from the following towns: Kununurra, Wyndham, Halls Creek, Fitzroy Crossing, Derby and Broome.

Sea

The *North Star* is a motor cruiser available for charter from Broome for a maximum of six guests. Information can be obtained from North Star Charters, PO Box 654, Broome, WA 6725. Tel. (091) 92 1829. Other vessels sometimes visit the Kimberley coast: contact any WA Tourist Centre.

Air

Scenic flights are run by commercial operators at the airports of: Broome, Derby, Fitzroy Crossing, Halls Creek, Wyndham and Kununurra. Float planes and helicopters can also be chartered at Kununurra and Broome. Helicopters can be chartered in Derby.

Tourist information

Information about the Kimberley and holiday bookings are available from WA Tourist Centres.

WA Tourism Commission
Head Office: 11th Floor, St Georges Court, 16 St Georges Terrace, Perth, WA 6000. Tel. (09) 220 1700.

WA Tourist Centre
772 Hay St, Perth, WA 6000. Tel. (09) 322 2999.

WA Tourist Centre
108 King William St, Adelaide, SA 5000. Tel. (08) 212 1344.

WA Tourist Centre
33 Elizabeth St, Melbourne, Vic. 3000. Tel. (03) 614 6833.

WA Tourist Centre,
92 Pitt St, Sydney, NSW 2000. Tel. (02) 233 4400.

WA Tourist Centre
Level 2, City Mutual Building, Brisbane, Qld 4000. Tel. (07) 229 5794.

Regional Tourist Offices in the Kimberley can provide more specific information. These are:

Broome Tourist Bureau
Great Northern Highway, Broome 6725. Tel. (091) 92 2222.

Derby Tourist Bureau
Clarendon St, Derby 6728. Tel. (091) 91 1426.

Halls Creek Tourism and Commercial Association
Great Northern Highway, Halls Creek 6770. Tel. (091) 68 6250.

Kununurra Visitors Centre
Coolibah Drive, Kununurra 6743. Tel. (091) 68 1177.

Wyndham Tourist Information Centre
O'Donnell Street, Wyndham Port 6741. Tel. (091) 61 1054.

Accommodation

Broome:
AUSKI Tropical Resort
Cable Beach Club
Continental Hotel
Overland Motor Inn
Mangrove Hotel
New Roebuck Bay Hotel
Roebuck Bay Resort

Derby:
West Kimberley Lodge
Derby Boab Inn
Kimberley Motor Inn
Spinifex Hotel
Willare Bridge Roadhouse

Fitzroy Crossing:
Crossing Motor Inn
Fitzroy River Lodge

Halls Creek:
Halls Creek Motel
Kimberley Hotel

Warmun Community:
Turkey Creek Lodge

Wyndham:
Wyndham Town Hotel

Kununurra:
Country Club, Kununurra Hotel,
Lake Argyle Inn, Kimberley Court,
Overland Motor Inn, Travellers
Guest House, Desert Inn,
Kununurra Backpackers.

There are caravan parks and
camping grounds in all the towns
listed above except Warmun
Community.

Dining out

There are restaurants or
cafés in all the towns with accommodation.

In general, food in the Kimberley is more expensive than
equivalent meals in more populated, accessible areas of Australia,
an inevitable result of the remote
nature of the region.

National Parks

The Kimberley regional office
of the Department of Conservation
and Land Management is at:
Messmate Way, Kununurra
(Regional Manager: Chris Done).
PO Box 942, Kununurra, WA 6743.
Tel. (091) 68 0200.

Shopping

The best things to buy in the
Kimberley are:

pearls (in Broome), Argyle diamonds (in Broome), zebra stone
jewellery (in Kununurra), decorative
sandstone ornaments (Kimberley
Colourstone, Derby), carved boab
nuts (Wyndham and elsewhere).

Aboriginal art – there are
specialist shops in Broome, Derby
and Kununurra and a roadside
stand in Fitzroy Crossing.

Broome: Goolarabooloo,
corner of Napier and Hamersley
Sts (PO Box 777, Broome, WA 6725).
Tel. (091) 921 804

Kununurra: Waringarri
Aboriginal Arts, Speargrass Rd
(PO Box 968, Kununurra, WA 6743).
Tel. (091) 682 212.

Time

Western Australian time is two
hours behind Eastern Standard
Time and one and a half hours
behind Central Standard Time.
There is no daylight saving.

Clothing

Dress in the Kimberley tends
to be very informal. Jackets and
ties are rarely required. Shorts are
generally acceptable but some
hotels may require that they be
worn with shoes and long socks.

Banks

Broome:
Commonwealth, Westpac,
R&I and agency of ANZ.
Derby:
ANZ and agencies of: Com-
monwealth Savings, NAB, R&I,
Westpac.
Fitzroy Crossing:
ANZ agency.
Halls Creek:
Agencies of: Commonwealth,
R&I and Westpac.
Wyndham:
R&I and agencies of National
and Commonwealth Banks.
Kununurra:
NAB, Commonwealth and
R&I.

Photography

The tropical sunlight in the
Kimberley is very strong. This
means that, as a general rule, you
can use slow-speed film. However,
you should avoid taking photographs that have part shade and
part sun because the shade parts
will turn out very dark and the well-
lit parts will be too bright. This can
be avoided in portraits by using a
flash to "fill in" the shadows.

Further reading

Mary Durack
Kings in Grass Castles
Sons in the Saddle

Ion L. Idriess
Outlaws of the Leopolds
Flynn of the Inland
In Crocodile Land
One Wet Season

Gordon Buchanan
Packhorse and Waterhole

Hugh Edwards
Port of Pearls

W.H. Tyler
Flight of Diamonds

Georg Walter PSM
Australia, Land, People, Mission

J.R.B. Love
Stone Age Bushmen of Today

G.H. Lamond
Tales of the Overland

Cathie Clement & P.J. Bridge
Kimberley Scenes (1989)
(a collection of diaries, letters,
etc., of the early days)

Malcolm Douglas
Follow the Sun

Index

Page numbers in bold type indicate the main reference.
Page numbers in italics indicate captions.

Photocredits

All photographs by Robbi Newman except:

Australian War Memorial Photograph 51741: 82
Hazel De Berg (courtesy National Library of Australia): 66
Malcolm Douglas: 28 (top), 33, 37, 61
Courtesy of Dame Mary Durack Miller: 60
Lorrie Graham: 151
Ron Hille: 34
Kevin Kenneally: all photographs on pages 140-41 except top far left
State Library of Victoria: 44
David McGonigal: 8-9, 13, 23, 28 (below), 32-33, 41 (below), 48 (left), 48 (below), 49, 57 (left), 64, 71, 75, 79, 81, 84, 94, 95, 99 (both), 103, 104-5, 105, 106, 107, 109, 110, 110-11, 112 (left), 113, 116, 117, 118-19, 123, 124, 124-5, 126, 127, 134-5, 142, 143, 150, 152
Mitchell Library, State Library of NSW: 50, 54, 57 (right)
National Library of Australia: 56, 58, 67, 77
National Library of Australia, Frank Johnston Collection: 76
National Library of Australia, Rex Nan Kivell Collection: 52, 53 (below), 55, 58-59
Dick Smith: 16 (right), 18, 62 (left), 73, 74, 77 (below), 114, 120, 121 (right), 130 (top), 146, 148, 153, 154-5
Pip Smith: 62 (right)
J. E. Stanton (courtesy of University of WA Anthropology Research Museum): 47 (top right)
Grahame L. Walsh: 47 (bottom row)
Howard Whelan: 3